The Real War on Terror

The Real War on Terror

Waging Holy War in the Peaceful Kingdom

By Derek Kubilus and Jon Priebe

Wipf & Stock
PUBLISHERS
Eugene, Oregon

To the many Christians who have carried the banner of Christ and his Kingdom before us, who did not love their lives, even when faced with death.

Contents

Acknowledgements

First, we'd like to thank and acknowledge God, who chose to save us and allow us to be a part of his kingdom. Only because of his grace have we been able to write this book.

We'd also like to thank Kattie Priebe, for her love and encouragement (and for giving up so many hours with her husband over these past months) and Daryl and Pat Kubilus for supporting their son with all his crazy ideas.

Special thanks also to the many others who helped and encouraged us, including Rabbi Moshe Adler, Doug Abel, Heather Pollock, Mike Wilson, Rev. Dave Scavuzzo, and Allen Roberts.

1

The Day Fear Invaded

"I hereby command you: Be strong and courageous; do not be frightened or dismayed, for the Lord your God is with you wherever you go." Joshua 1:9

THE WORLD honorably wages war in search of peace. Throughout all of history, humankind has fought in vain against itself, hoping that peace would somehow come from the blood sacrificed by millions of women, children, and men. Theologians, philosophers, and soldiers have long theorized and speculated on how to make war to achieve peace. They think that if only they can wrest control from this last dictator, if only they can win this last war, there will be peace. They think. They hope. But then, as always, another iron-fisted tyrant springs up in some other nation or a band of religious extremists decides to fly planes into crowded buildings, and once again, it appears necessary to strike down evildoers who threaten the safety of the innocent.

Despite thousands of years of war-making "for peace," true and lasting peace still eludes us. Humanity has not yet learned this inescapable lesson: *war only begets more war, and violence only begets more violence.* Those eleven words fully summarize the teachings of the entire history of warfare. The cycle of fear and retaliation cannot be broken with bloodshed. No, the only remedy for this disease of never-ending violence that has plagued humanity since Cain killed Abel is for us to rise above the violence itself, to transcend the fear that compels us to take up arms against one another, and to overcome evil with good.[1]

We, Jon and Derek, have come to the realization that all this war and violence is completely and utterly incompatible with Christ's teaching. We have discovered that God, through his eternal Word, has shown his children a better way, a higher path. We believe that through Christ, God has taught us that violence is not the answer to overcoming the world's

1. Rom 12:21.

I

problems and that his children should abstain from *all* violence and, instead, lead lives of peace and self-sacrifice.

We humbly ask for your time. On paper, two twenty-somethings from the Midwest have very little credibility on this theological issue. But we realize that God often works through those with very little or no credibility. Moses, David, Jesus . . . all were nothing in the eyes of man. We surely don't place ourselves in their company, but we pray that God would use us, like he used them, to convey a small portion of his Word . . . that through this book, we could play a minor role in the building of Christ's peaceable Kingdom. We only ask that you approach this work with a humble heart and a discerning mind. As you read our discussion of nonviolence, we urge you to search the Scriptures to test what we say. Don't take what we say for granted. Think for yourself; push into God; fearlessly search out the truth.

We are not the first folks to have come to the conclusion that evil cannot overcome evil and that violence cannot create an enduring peace. Ancient Greek playwrights, Indian mystics, American Civil Rights pioneers, and yes, even Evangelical Christians have proposed this same view over the years. It's just that we've noticed that this perspective often gets dismissed and ridiculed as cowardice. Therefore, it is often confined to college philosophy texts, seminary libraries, and Phish concerts. We want to bring this position back to where it belongs: in the mainstream of Christianity. We want nonviolence to be taught in our Sunday schools and preached about from our pulpits. This book is intended to be a stepping stone for bringing the issue of nonviolence back to the front lines of Christian ethics.

Given the political climate that our nation finds itself in, as well as the violence that plagues our streets, Christians in America cannot afford to ignore the issue of violence. As elected officials wage war on our behalf, spending our tax dollars on weapons to kill enemies who could be called to repentance, our spiritual shepherds remain silent. According to a Pew Forum study from March 2003, only fifty-seven percent of American pastors had recently spoken on the issue of war with Iraq. Unbelievably, only a third of those who had discussed the topic were concerned enough for their flock to take a position on war (for or against).[2] How can Christians remain silent while terrorists hurl threats against us, our money is used to finance a war against those terrorists, and our sons and daughters are being sent into harms way, all in the name of national defense? War is a reality.

2. Pew Forum on Religion and Public Life, *Different Faiths, Different Messages.*

We Christians must acknowledge this and search for a Christian response to it.

General William Tecumseh Sherman once wrote, "War is hell."[3] Americans now know this all too well. Only six short years ago, America was shocked out of her complacency to find that she still lives in a world where war and violence are grim realities. In September of 2001, it became apparent that although this "hell" that Sherman mentioned had long been relegated to history books and international news broadcasts, war can still reach our seemingly secure back yards and change our ways of life forever.

Most Americans would agree that the attacks of September 11th have had a profound impact on their lives. The vast majority of Americans are still able to tell you where they were and what they were doing on that bright Tuesday morning. Not since the assassination of John F. Kennedy or the Challenger explosion has the nation felt such a connection to a particular day. Millions of opinions about war and violence have been forged from the smoldering ruins of the Twin Towers. This invasion left many feeling scared, some angry, but it left almost all, including us, feeling very confused.

Derek's September 11 Experience

That morning was like any other. Coffee in hand, I showed up at the office, but for some reason, no one was at their desks. I just figured our Wednesday team meeting had been bumped up to Tuesday and that I had not gotten the memo. So I went to the conference room, where I found the entire office crowded around a television set, watching the towers burning.

"When the first one hit, everyone thought it was just an accident, but then a second plane took out the other tower!" exclaimed a coworker with a bewildered look on her face. It was apparent that this was no accident. This was an act of aggression the likes of which no one in Generation X had ever seen before.

The following week was almost surreal. Government officials were making constant statements, crews were working around the clock to find survivors, and images of sobbing families were plastered all over the news. There were people missing work all over the place and coworkers were

---

3. General Sherman commanded one of the largest Union armies through the deep South toward the end of the American Civil War. Sherman and his army pillaged and destroyed plantation after plantation across the Shenandoah River valley.

found crying at their desks. For the very first time in my life, I found myself mourning for people I didn't even know. Something had shaken us up and jarred us from our comfortable lives in Western society.

For the first time in several decades, we felt vulnerable as a nation. We all felt like victims. We were all faced with the horrific reality that we could die an untimely death at the hands of another at any moment.

I suppose that's why we all flocked to church that Sunday. Many in our nation had never seriously dealt with the issue of death before. Many never considered that the chaotic violence that was so prevalent on television broadcasts from other countries could *actually be real!* No one believed it could ever come to into our nation and touch our lives. We all found ourselves playing a role we were not accustomed to. Americans were faced with their own mortality, and they wanted to see what God had to say. In this grand play called human existence, Americans found themselves playing the part of the helpless victim for the first time, and we needed to know why.

I guess we could all identify with Jesus at that moment. He was a man of supreme power, capable of creating and destroying worlds with a single word. He drove out demons, healed the blind and walked on water. Yet, even in his power, he found himself playing the role of the victim, being crucified on a cross. So it was with the United States. We are a nation of supreme power. America basically controls the world's economy, protects smaller nations with its nuclear arsenal, and topples oppressive governments, all in our spare time. How could America, like Jesus, fall at the hands of those who were so weak in comparison?

The absurdity of the situation was too much for most to handle. Starting with church services on September 16th, the people of this great, yet vulnerable nation called for war. This injustice could not be allowed to stand. America must save face.

I was surprised when I heard this message preached at church that Sunday. It wasn't that I disagreed with that message. It's just that I had grown accustomed to pastors talking about compassion, loving your enemies, and all that. It was unsettling to hear sentiments of war and vengeance being preached in front of the altar of God.

At that moment I first recognized that there was some tension between the concept of war and the teachings of Jesus Christ. I already knew it was there in the back of my mind, but I had never really focused on it before. Just as quickly as I came to that realization I decided to table that thought, putting it back on the rear burner for another day. I needed to focus on freedom, loyalty and the flag that represented those things. I had no time or energy to devote to complex ethical deliberation.

But as time went on and we began attacking the Taliban in Afghanistan, I found it more and more difficult to stop thinking about resolving the conflict between Christ's Sermon on the Mount and the practice of war. Part of me was calmed by seeing war taking place where it belonged: on television in a foreign land. But, another part of me was just starting to stir. It was as if a different side of me was just now waking up for the first time, and that it was rubbing its eyes, asking, "What's going on?"

Over the next year or two, as the war waged on in Afghanistan and a new war "to defend freedom" was being spoken of, I started asking myself if I should be in support of such action, even though on the outside I would never let on that I had any doubts. Even as freedom was established in Afghanistan and the new battle in the "war on terror" was beginning with "shock and awe," I had the unsettling feeling that something very devious and malevolent was at work in our midst. Every time I heard "God Bless America" sung at a baseball game, every time I saw another telethon to support the victims of the attacks, every time I saw a "These Colors Don't Run" bumper sticker, I felt more and more confused. It was as if the whole world was going mad, and I was just starting to realize it.

Jon's September 11 Experience

When the attacks of September 11th happened, I was lifting weights at the gym. The radio station interrupted a song to announce that there had been an explosion at the WTC buildings in New York. Curious, I wrapped up my weights routine and hopped onto an exercise bike in the cardio room where I could watch television. As I watched live coverage of the first tower burning, the second plane collided with the other tower. I was scared, yet I felt oddly distant from the attacks. It was almost like I was watching a movie or a news report from some other country, not an actual event in America. As I wrapped up my workout, I called my boss at work. They still wanted us to come in. Darn, an unexpected day off would've been nice.

That afternoon, while I was at work, my brother left me a voicemail. John Hart, a man from our church, was in the World Trade Center buildings at the time of the attacks and his wife hadn't heard from him since a cell phone call right after the impacts. John and his family had been a part of my church during my teenage years. When I was in high school, I spent many Sunday afternoons playing flag football with the guys from our church, including John and his oldest step-son. He worked at a regional bank in Ohio until they downsized his business unit. A few months after he left the bank, John moved his family to California to pursue a job offer. He was in the World Trade Center buildings that Tuesday because he was on a business trip for his new employer.

It shook me up to think that this kind and gentle man, that I knew personally, might be gone forever. At 21, I had only rarely had to deal with the death of someone that I knew well. Now that the attacks had struck a personal note, I started to give serious thought to what had happened and what it meant. Weeks passed and I watched the news coverage of the wars starting in Afghanistan and then later in Iraq. I was glad we were protecting America. I hoped we would find Bin-Laden and bring him to justice! I was ready to fight if America needed me. At the time, I was working full time and enrolled in college part time. Though my patriotism urged me to fight, I was still in school, so I decided that I would only enlist if we ever came up short on troops.

Before too long, though, the swelling of patriotism within me began to cause some discomfort. I heard and saw reports of the alleged misconduct of our troops overseas. I was saddened by the news of the prison abuse at the Guantanamo Bay detainment camp and Abu Ghraib prison. Frequently, I'd look over the ever-lengthening list of our dead and wounded troops, hoping to not see the names of my friends who were fighting in Iraq. Slowly, I began to question some things: Why do we need to make the Middle East democratic? Why is Democracy worth killing the fathers and sons of Afghanistan and Iraq? Are these wars more about protecting ourselves and our interests, or are we actually fighting for the Afghanis and Iraqis?

My questions had many would-be answer-ers. There were those like filmmaker Michael Moore who told me that the wars were all about oil and American imperialism. U.S. and British politicians said that Democracy was best for all the nations of the world and that it was our responsibility to give it to them. Some conservative Christian writers like Chuck Colson wanted us to believe that the wars were about Christian charity. Popular opinion seemed to hint that these wars were about revenge for September 11th and Saddam Hussein attempting to assassinate George H. W. Bush. I even heard a song on the radio claiming that the American way to respond to the terrorists would be to put our boot in their ass.

After finding these answers insufficient and a little unpleasant, I turned to Scripture. In retrospect, I should have consulted our Lord's words a little sooner. Nonetheless, what I found in the words of Jesus and Paul was very different than what others were saying. Weeks turned to months as I read, studied, prayed, and talked with other folks who sought answers to these same questions.

The *Real* War on Terror

As you can see, the attacks and the subsequent retaliation on the part of the United States drove us to start thinking about war and its compatibility with the teachings of our Lord, Jesus Christ. All our lives we simply accepted what we were taught about violence. It made perfect sense that violence was necessary in some cases to protect the weak and the innocent. We had never before realized just how little we chewed on the messages that were being fed to us before we swallowed them.

In subtle ways we are being told not to challenge such beliefs. The bumper stickers, the army commercials, the military tributes at ball games, the yellow alert . . . all reinforce the idea that violence is necessary to defend the freedoms we all enjoy. Slowly we are being evangelized with the gospel of war, and most of us accept it without much deliberation. Peace is the goal, they say, but bloodshed has to be the means.

It is undeniable that the 9/11 attacks and the war on terror have created a peculiar and uncomfortable social climate. Do you remember the anthrax-scares of October 2001? Several letters, laced with anthrax and sent to senators and media figures, triggered a nationwide postal scare. Americans panicked. Just as we were returning to a sense of normalcy, we were threatened once again by an anonymous enemy who could target any one of us at any time.

The terror continued: In December 2001, Richard Reid was caught trying to light a bomb in his shoe while riding in an airplane. November 2001, it was announced that an attack was planned against the Golden Gate Bridge. In May 2002, Jose Padilla was arrested for conspiracy to commit murder with a so-called "dirty bomb" which could have exposed millions to radiation poisoning. Late in the summer of 2005 a panic broke out in New York City as word came that our subways were being targeted. We were told that scores of terror cells had been uncovered, and not just in our nation's most populated cities. Five orange alerts from March 2002 to May 2004 kept us "vigilant" and suspicious of our neighbors. Everywhere we turned, every television station, every politician, every newspaper screamed, and still screams, the same message: *We must be afraid!*

But must we be afraid? Must we live our lives in perpetual anxiety over the next possible attack? NO! The Truth, the Gospel message, directly contradicts this message of fear that has been force-fed to us over the past 5 years: Jesus tells us "Do not fear those who kill the body but cannot kill the soul; Rather fear him who can destroy both soul and body in hell."[4]

Obeying fear makes us lose perspective. When our fears are left unchecked, we become completely fixated on all the things that could possibly harm or destroy us. Fear activates our animal instincts, demanding that we do anything and everything in our power to save ourselves and our loved ones. Fear would even have us compromise what we believe for the sake of our selves and our safety.

All this worry causes us to forget that we have a perfectly sovereign God, at whose command the entire universe came into existence. It is upon his strength, not our own, that we must lean when fear starts to creep its way into our daily lives. As Paul wrote to Timothy, "For God did not give us a spirit of cowardice, but rather a spirit of power, love, and self-discipline."[5] It is with love, hard work and the power of the Holy Spirit that we must combat the "rulers, the authorities and the cosmic forces of this present darkness"[6] which sponsor the fear that pervades our society. They want us to be afraid, but we know that fear is opposite of faith. As Christians, faith is everything to us, and therefore, we cannot afford to be afraid.

On October 6, 2005 at the National Endowment for Democracy, President Bush said, "We will not tire, or rest, until the War on Terror is won." As Christians, we are called to the same battle cry. The difference is that we are called to fight the terror itself, not the terrorists. We are called to combat the fear itself, not those we fear. We must battle hatred itself, not those we hate. We wage war on Evil himself, not just human evildoers. Truly, a Christian's struggle is *not* against flesh and blood.[7]

Waging Holy War

We fully understand that the nonviolent position is often labeled as "idealistic." We'd agree that it can easily be seen as such. The nonviolent Christian lifestyle that we proclaim, that Jesus proclaimed, requires choices that common-sense practicality considers simply ridiculous. The problem is that popular American Christianity has *lost its sense* of the ridiculous. We have strayed from the radical ideas that Christ and the Apostles taught and died for. We're too worried about real estate appreciation and the

4. Matt 10:28.

5. 2 Tim 1:7.

6. Eph 6:12.

7. Eph 6:12.

stock market to risk the radical lifestyle that Jesus called us to. We have forgotten that when Paul urged the Roman church to "confess with your lips that Jesus is Lord,"[8] he was encouraging them to risk their lives by publicly claiming allegiance to Jesus instead of Caesar. This public faith could easily have landed them in a first-century Roman prison or on an executioner's block.

Perhaps to become more attractive, popular Christianity has brought into itself the sensible, atheistic teachings of the faithless world around it. This world teaches Christians that before all else, we must pursue our own safety and that of our family. This world teaches us that we must take our safety into our own hands, raising up walls and armies around our loved ones to protect them from the ever-present enemies that seek only to destroy and plunder. This world teaches us that "life" is the only thing we have and that therefore it must be defended at all costs. Physical safety and bodily health have become the objectives of the Christian life. In stark contrast stands the message of our Messiah: eternal safety and spiritual health.

Consider Paul the Apostle, the first missionary to the Greek and Roman world. In the course of his service to God, he was beaten, whipped, stoned, thrice shipwrecked and at one point, adrift in the Mediterranean for 36 hours.[9] He fully understood that God calls us up *out* of the safety we have surrounded ourselves with and *into* the security of his call. Paul knew that living a life of faith meant living a life of danger and foolishness before men.[10] Paul could see that he, like all Christians, was called out from his comfortable lifestyle to seek out the "dangerous" life God had in store for him.

Christian nonviolence is not about safety. It is not about protecting our lives and our families. It is not about making fair and just societies where people can enjoy physical freedoms and the right to live as they please. Nonviolence is about the O-word, this nine-letter word that seldom rings from pulpits today. Obedience. It is about submitting to the sovereign, providential call of God. It is about living radical lives of discipleship, fighting the good fight of the faith, winning souls, and redeeming the world through peacemaking.

Christian nonviolence starts from the understanding that seeking safety through violence is vanity. It is a delusion to believe that the re-

8. Rom 10:9.
9. 2 Cor 11:35.
10. 1 Cor 1:22–25

demption of the world can be achieved through violence, which is itself a corruption of God-given power. If we are to live authentic Christian lives, we must cleanse ourselves of the need for safety and begin to understand that all Christians are called to put themselves on the line, risking their lives and their physical safety for God's Kingdom on Earth. In short, we must wage war against God's enemies: the self and the ideologies of this world. We must forsake our bodies as Christ forsook his.

Our Clear Objective

For any war to be successful, the soldiers must be given a clear objective. The clearest communication of our objective as Christians comes from the lips of Christ in Matthew's Gospel, "Go therefore and make disciples of all nations, baptizing them in the name of the Father and of the Son and of the Holy Spirit, and teaching them to obey everything that I have commanded you."[11]

All humanity has sinned against God. We are all complicit in the sin of Adam and Eve. We have all traded God's law for our own, insisting that we know how best to run our lives. This has plunged humanity into a state of depravity and seemingly endless violence. Don't take our word for it, though. Take a look for yourself at one day's worth of news headlines. We are surrounded with rape, murder, theft, adultery and fraud. Additionally, Jesus tells us that to even think adulterous thoughts and to hold hatred in our hearts is equivalent to the actual sins of adultery and murder![12] Under this new law that Christ gave in the Sermon on the Mount, aren't we all murderers and adulterers at heart?! Paul summarized the news headlines of his world this way: "All have sinned and fall short of the glory of God."[13]

Leading lives of sin causes much unnecessary fear to enter our lives. Like Adam, we become scared of God's presence, fearing punishment for breaking his law. This fear causes us to run farther from God, which in turn leads us further down our dark path of disobedience, which causes more fear and so on. This cycle of fear and flight makes us all enemies with God.

Graciously, God has provided a way out of this vicious cycle. From his compassion was born Jesus of Nazareth, his Son. Jesus taught and showed us the way of faith and died a horrific, embarrassing death. His sacrifice paid the price for our sin and showed us the way of faithful obedience,

11. Matt 28:19–20.

12. Matt 5: 21–28.

13. Rom 3:23.

which takes away the fear of death through God's granting of eternal life. We no longer need to fear retribution and condemnation for our sins. Impossibly, God has granted us pardon; in turn, he asks us to show others the way to his Son.

When Robert E. Lee surrendered to Ulysses S. Grant at Appomattox Court House on April 5, 1865, the American Civil War was officially over. Victory had been won by the Union. The slaughter of American men (Christians) by their brother Americans (also Christians!) could finally stop. Unfortunately, the news of this victory did not spread quickly. For weeks and even months Union and Confederate troops skirmished across the southeastern United States. On the seas and in some outlying areas of the still barren West, fighting continued for nearly three months. The good news of the end of the war did not spread quickly enough. The messengers could only reach so far, so fast. So also, the fight of the Christian is to spread the good news that the war has been won and God's peace has been poured out.

By making disciples of all nations, we are spreading word of God's reconciliation and the good news that we need not fear death, for Jesus overcame death itself on the cross. "Oh death, where is your victory? Oh death, where is your sting? The sting of death is sin, and the power of sin is the law; but thanks be to God, who gives us the victory through our Lord, Jesus Christ." [14] The war has already been won. Our marching orders, then, are to declare the victory of Christ over the power of fear. We must spread the good news that the fight is won and peace with God is available for those who ask.

Our Sole Enemy

Before an army can lay out its goals based on its objectives, its enemy must be identified. The Church has often had trouble with this very basic concept. Jews, Muslims, witches, abortion doctors, homosexuals, and even Socialists have all been mistakenly identified as enemies of Christ. It seems that the Church has forgotten the words of Paul: "our struggle is not against enemies of flesh and blood." [15] Our battle is against the devil, the ruler of this age, who has "blinded the minds of the unbelievers, to keep them from seeing the light of the gospel of the glory of Christ." [16] Satan has blinded us and supplanted the faith in God we were all given with his

14. 1 Cor 15:55–57.
15. Eph 6:12.
16. 2 Cor 4:4.

evil ideology of hate, self-interest, and idolatry. For centuries, Christians have been beating against the wind as we've struggled in vain against those whom we have been commissioned to love, not realizing that our enemy cannot be beaten with weapons of war.

We heard a story of a Muslim woman being baptized into Christ's body. She had accepted God's grace through Christ after experiencing the non-judgmental, non-controlling, unconditional love of a Christian. This woman would likely have been *killed* by eleventh century European Christians.

By being a witness of Christ's love to this woman, the Christian soldier won a victory over the ideologies of this world. This Christian woman chose not to fight against the person who represented a different worldview than her own. The Christian witness understood that her enemy could not be fought with violence, but could only be overcome through love.

The battle this Christian fought was not waged on a grassy plain, or on a sandy beach. Rather, she fought through a web of hurt and depression, expressing unconditional love to tear down the spiritual and emotional strongholds in the Muslim woman's heart and mind. This is the theatre of our war: the hearts and minds of those held captive by the "cosmic powers of this present darkness."[17]

As we fight this spiritual battle on a spiritual battleground, we need to protect ourselves with spiritual defenses and arm ourselves with spiritual weapons. We can't expect to fight this war with M16's, Kevlar vests, and Patriot missiles. Thankfully, Paul had the inspired foresight to teach us about the weapons and armor of a soldier of Christ, as he saw it:

> Be strong in the Lord and in the strength of his power. Put on the whole armor of God, so that you may be able to stand against the wiles of the devil. For our struggle is not against enemies of blood and flesh, but against the rulers, against the authorities, against the cosmic powers of this present darkness, against the spiritual forces of evil in the heavenly places. Therefore take up the whole armor of God, so that you may be able to withstand on that evil day, and having done everything, to stand firm. Stand therefore, and fasten the belt of truth around your waist, and put on the breastplate of righteousness. As shoes for your feet put on whatever will make you ready to proclaim the gospel of peace. With all of these, take the shield of faith, with which you will be able to quench all the

17. Eph 6:12.

flaming arrows of the evil one. Take the helmet of salvation, and the sword of the Spirit, which is the word of God.[18]

"In the final analysis, discipleship is a life of sublime madness," wrote Brennan Manning.[19] The army of God fights for the hearts and minds of the world, clothed in Truth, Righteousness, Peace, Salvation, and armed only with the Holy Spirit. From the outside, our behavior must seem like madness. We return good when given evil, we forgive those who harm us, and we do good to those who could never return the favor. We're ridiculous, just as our Master was ridiculous. But, "Blessed are you when people revile you and persecute you . . . Rejoice and be glad, for your reward is great in heaven, for in the same way they persecuted the prophets before you."[20]

18. Eph 6:10–7.
19. Manning, *The Ragamuffin Gospel*, 192.
20. Matt 5:11–12.

2

The Lord Is a Warrior

"'Not by might, nor by power; but by my spirit,' says the Lord of hosts." Zechariah 4:6

ONE SUNDAY morning, one of us overheard an interesting conversation between two ladies before their Sunday school class. On that particular Sunday, their class was scheduled to discuss Genesis 22. In this chapter, God instructs Abraham to sacrifice Isaac, his son. When Abraham's wife, Sarah, was unable to conceive, God had promised to give them a son. Isaac was the fulfillment of that promise. Though God stops him as he is bringing the knife down, he blesses Abraham for not withholding his only son.[1] Neither of the two ladies could understand why God would demand such a violent thing from Abraham and subsequently bless him for actually doing it. "That's why I don't read the Old Testament," one of them said, "it paints a very violent and mean picture of God, not at all like Jesus in the New Testament."

Their sentiment is very common, too common, in the church today. A major fault of the American church is our over-reliance on the New Testament. There is a false sentiment that Jesus somehow replaced the God who revealed himself through the Hebrew Scriptures. We do agree that the New Testament Scriptures are foundational to Christian life, since they chronicle the life, death and resurrection of our Lord. However, the Church's focus on these newer writings often causes us to forget that Jesus was actually Jewish. He knew the Hebrew Bible inside and out. He memorized the prophets. He would have known that he was the completion and the fulfillment of all of God's actions and promises in the Old Testament. He is the full revelation of God.[2] There is no division or difference between the "God of the Old Testament" and Jesus. The "God of the Old

1. Gen 22:12.
2. John 14:9; Col 1:19.

Testament" is the Father, and Jesus is his son; they are indispensable to each other. In order to fully understand the Father, we must understand Jesus; in order to understand Jesus, we must understand the Father, the "God of the Old Testament."

The Old Testament is more than the ramblings of an ancient and violent race of people with an inaccurate view of God. No, it is still the divine revelation of Yahweh, the Word of God, useful for teaching, reproof, correction and training in righteousness.[3] For several hundred years before the birth of Jesus, it was humanity's only written revelation from God. Christ quoted it, Paul quoted it, and so should we, even though we are nonviolent. For nonviolence to be an acceptable Christian position, it *must* be able to account for the violence of the Old Testament. We cannot ignore the Old Testament as the two ladies above so easily did. If we dare claim that the nonviolence that Jesus preached is meant to be the stance for Christians, we should be able to show that both God's commands to the Israelites to use violence and the words of the prophets point the way for Christians to become nonviolent.

Firstly, however, we would like to correct the very popular, but misplaced belief that God loves or even approves of human violence. Nothing could be further from the truth. As we mentioned earlier, Cain is the first example of human violence in the Bible. God hated the fact that Cain murdered his brother! Because of Cain's violence, God actually cursed the ground to become unfruitful and banished Cain to an even more desolate place than he had banished his parents, Adam and Eve.[4]

Cain's violence multiplied and intensified over the generations that followed him until Lamech, Cain's great-grandson, killed a boy just for hitting him![5] This is a prime example of how violence will always multiply and intensify over time. Future generations *will* learn violence when their parents are violent. As we said, violence only begets more violence. If the world is to have any true hope for peace, this cycle must be broken. We who follow Christ must set a model of reconciliation, not revenge, for our sons and daughters to emulate.

The cycle of violence, started by Cain and sped up by Lamech, spread like wildfire through the earliest civilization. As we can see in Genesis 6, violence was as popular as ever: "Now the earth was corrupt in God's sight

3. 2 Tim 3:16.

4. Gen 4:9–12.

5. Gen 4:23.

and the earth was filled with violence."[6] In fact, God said that his sole purpose for destroying the world with a flood during the time of Noah was that it had been spoiled by violence! "I have determined to make an end of all flesh," said God, "because the earth is filled with violence because of them; now I am going to destroy them along with the earth."[7] You see, God hated the violence of the world and he recognized that the world had become practically irredeemable because of it. God couldn't even work with this ancient world any longer, as they had defiled themselves with violence to a point that they were no longer even capable of receiving the grace of God.

For another example of God's distaste for violence, consider David, called, "a man after God's own heart."[8] Though he wanted to build God's temple in Jerusalem, he was not allowed because he had shed too much blood. David had made a career fighting "The Lord's battles."[9] However, God would not allow him to build the temple. It was too holy and David's hands were too stained by blood.[10] Though he deemed it necessary in a few instances in the Hebrew Scriptures, God's holiness still causes him to be displeased by human violence. He wanted a man of peace, Solomon, to lay the bricks of the temple.[11] Today, Christians are the building blocks of God's spiritual house, his new temple.[12] If a man stained by violence could not be allowed to build that temple, how could men and women who use violence today *be* the temple of God?

Perhaps the clearest place in the Hebrew Scriptures where we hear of God's distaste for violence is the psalms. "The Lord tests the righteous and the wicked, and his soul hates the lover of violence."[13] Violence is depicted as a primary characteristic of wickedness and God sets his soul against those who love it.

"But Jon, Derek, come on guys. Hardly anyone *loves* violence. Even soldiers and generals recognize that violence is a terrible, yet necessary evil. No one wants for there to be violence, but evil actions necessitate a swift, sometimes violent response." Well, we don't really buy the claim

---

6. Gen 6:11.

7. Gen 6:13.

8. 1 Sam 13:13–14; Acts 13:22.

9. 1 Sam 25:28.

10. 1 Chr 22:8.

11. 1 Chr 22:9.

12. 1 Cor 3:16–17, 6:19; 1 Pet 2:5.

13. Ps 11:5.

that hardly anyone loves violence. For example, the military must train its personnel to enjoy and even love what they are trained to do. Think about it: if your sole source of income, your job, and your purpose in life is to make violence, before long most of us will begin to develop a dependence, a fondness, and eventually a devout love for violence.

But the love of violence has spread beyond soldiers alone. Just look at the ways we entertain ourselves. Some of our most eagerly awaited summer blockbusters are violent action movies, raking in hundreds of millions of dollars. In 2004 the top two video games sold were Grand Theft Auto: San Andreas and Halo 2. In Grand Theft Auto, players are awarded points for stealing cars, hitting pedestrians, and killing police officers. In Halo 2, a game that one of us basically wasted an entire summer playing, the sole objective of the game is to seek out and destroy fellow players. Now, we know that most people who play these video games and go to action movies don't go out and rob banks or shoot their friends, but that's not our point. Our point is that we Americans have a certain affinity (would we dare say "love") for violence.

Adonai Ish Milchama—The Lord is a warrior

Despite all this, God does command, approve of, and carry out an awful lot of violence in the Hebrew Scriptures. Even in the above story from Genesis 6, it is God himself who floods the earth, destroying nearly every man, woman, child and animal on the face of the planet. How can a God who wishes to solve the problem of war and violence on earth do so by making more violence? Weren't God's actions even more brutal than the violence he was fighting against?

If we look to the book of Exodus it seems like we see an equally aggressive God raining down plagues upon Egypt, causing many deaths. Among these was the final plague, where God struck down the first born of every house of Egypt. The vicious ferocity of this final plague was too much for Pharaoh, and he allowed the Hebrew slaves to go free. After some time, however, Pharaoh's heart became hardened against the Hebrews and he sent his army after them. In defense of his people, God miraculously parts the waters to let the Israelites go through. Just as easily, he brings the waters of the Red Sea down upon Pharaoh's army, completely wiping out the entire Egyptian army in one fell swoop. In response to God's violent protection of his people, Moses sings out a song of praise, calling God a warrior, an *Ish Milchama*.[14]

14. Exod 15:2.

This theme of God protecting his people through violence is not only limited to these two stories, however. In fact, there is said to be an entire book, now lost, of Hebrew poetry that speaks of the "Wars of Yahweh."[15] Also, God is often seen rescuing and fighting for the Psalm writers. For example, "The Lord is my rock and my fortress and my deliverer . . . I call upon the Lord, who is worthy to be praised, so I shall be saved from my enemies,"[16] and, "Who is the King of Glory? The Lord, strong and mighty, the Lord, mighty in battle."[17]

So why does a violent God demand nonviolence from his people? Why would God talk so badly about human violence and in the next moment use violence against humanity? The Psalmist proclaims the answer: "The Lord looks down from heaven on humankind to see if there are any who are wise, who seek after God. They have all gone astray, they are all alike perverse; there is no one who does good, no, not one."[18] God alone has the proper authority, perspective, and moral standing to execute wrath. Like Cain and Lamech, our intellects are clouded by sins like pride and greed. Just as Lamech killed a boy to protect his pride when the boy simply hit him, so we repay more than what was suffered. We are too finite and too stained by the world to be entrusted with the authority to make war on our own.

Perhaps this is why God inspired the author of Proverbs to write, "Do not say, 'I will repay evil'; wait for the LORD, and he will help you."[19] Paul seems to be referring to this Scripture when he says, "Beloved, never avenge yourselves, but leave room for the wrath of God; for it is written 'Vengeance is mine, I will repay,' says the Lord."[20] You see, we cannot be trusted with vengeance. We cannot be trusted to defend ourselves. Our attempts at self defense and rightful vengeance turn into undue aggression and unreasonable revenge. Think of all the road rage cases we hear about in America these days. Is shooting at someone really an appropriate response to getting cut off on the highway?

We make a mess of these things because we are blinded by our own pain and pride. Only God has the eternal perspective and the righteous wisdom, born from his omniscience, which are needed to execute this

---

15. Num 21:14.

16. Ps 18: 2–3.

17. Ps 24:8.

18. Ps 14:2–3.

19. Prov 20:22.

20. Rom 12:19.

kind of judgment. We must wait, trusting him who knows and sees all things to be our champion, our warrior, our *Ish Milchama*.

God is a General

Along with being a mighty warrior *for* his people, there are times when God is the wise and seasoned general *of* his people. Yes, there are times in the Old Testament where God uses people as instruments of his judgment to wage war on evildoers. However, there are two very important things that Christians must understand about these events in Jewish history: 1) God typically does most of the fighting himself, and 2) God expects his people to follow very strict and often unorthodox orders in each military campaign.

When God teaches his people how to wage war, it is based on his heavenly perspective, even when his strategy makes no earthly sense. Consider the siege of Jericho, Joshua's first battle after the crossing of the Jordan.[21] The Israelites were commanded to attack Jericho, but when they arrived, they discovered that the walls were too high and thick to be easily destroyed. God gave the Israelite army hope, though, commanding them to march around the walls of the city for seven days and then to shout and make a loud noise. If they would do this, God would tear down the walls for them. When they obeyed his ridiculous order, God flattened the walls of Jericho for them, handing Joshua the battle!

Imagine being a soldier in Joshua's army. Imagine hearing your commander tell you that you had to march around the walls of a city for a whole week and then act like a fool, making strange noises and shouting. Imagine how much faith in God it would take to make you fight a battle like that! This is the kind of faith that is required for nonviolence and the radical discipleship it implies.

An even better example of the ridiculous orders God gives is the story of Gideon in the book of Judges. Gideon is told by God to reduce the size of his army from 32,000 men to 300 men. So that the people of Israel would not forget that God alone delivers them from danger, Gideon had to defeat the entire Midianite army with one percent of his original fighting force.[22] As Gideon and his men approach, God confuses the enemy so that they start mistakenly killing each other. The rout is on and the victory won before the rest of the Israelite army even shows up.[23] Here again, we

21. Josh 6:20.
22. Judg 7:1–7.
23. Judg 7:19–25.

see God fighting the wars of those who have enough faith to obey his ridiculous commands.

Both of those examples were from the Israelite war against the Canaanites who occupied the land that God had promised them. There are several other accounts of God's faithfulness to his army from those campaigns.[24] But how about during the monarchy of Israel and Judah? During Jehoshaphat's reign, an army of men from three neighboring kingdoms invaded the Promised Land. The people asked for help and God, their warrior, responded. "Do not fear or be dismayed at this great multitude, for the battle is not yours but God's," he told them.[25] God would destroy the enemy; they only needed to go out and stand by as he did the fighting. Jehoshaphat and his army obeyed, standing by and singing praise songs to God. As they watched, God made the three other armies wipe each other out. Through their obedience, Jehoshaphat's army didn't lose a single soldier.

The Problem of Obedience

However, not all of Israel's history is filled with tales of obedience to God's odd commands during warfare. The book of Judges reports one such instance where soldiers in God's army didn't do what they were told. God gave the Israelites strict instructions to drive out the people they found in the Promised Land.[26] God knew best, because he sits outside of time and could see all the problems that would be caused if these peoples were allowed to stay with the Israelites. But they did not listen. They felt that the Canaanites did not need to all die, some would better serve as slaves.[27] However, the Canaanite women ended up causing the Israelites to slip into idolatry with their false idols. God had warned them that the people from the Promised Land would become a thorn in their flesh if they were allowed to stay and the next 350 years proved God right.[28] Israel fought war after war with these people that they should have driven out or destroyed.

Another interesting lesson in obedience to God's demands for nonviolence comes from a very unusual source: post-Jesus Judaism. A few years after Gaius Caligula became emperor in 37 AD, he sent an army, under

24. Josh 10:14, 10:42, 23:3.
25. 2 Chr 20:15.
26. Nums 33:51–56.
27. Judg 1:28.
28. Num 33:55.

a man named Petronius, with strict orders to erect statues of Caligula in Jerusalem. If anyone complained or rebelled, they were to be executed. But rebel they did, although they did so nonviolently. A large number of Jews met the army in a field outside a city in Galilee. They told Petronius that if he wanted to erect statues of Caesar, he would first have to kill their entire race. It was more important to them that they obey God and potentially be killed, than to compromise their obedience and remain alive.

Petronius stalled to notify Caligula of the faithful devotion of the Jewish people and their dedication to obey God. However, before the messengers could get back to Rome to obtain the Emperor's response, news came to Judea that Caligula was dead. With his death, the edict requiring the statues to be built was nullified. Nonviolence had helped the Jews avoid war.[29]

But, this peace did not last. Over the next twenty-five years, the region's political stability deteriorated under several corrupt Roman governors. Then, in May 66, the Jewish people revolted. They'd had enough of Roman oppression and corruption. It was time to fight to regain their rights to govern themselves and worship as God had intended. They would not compromise their divine commandments by worshipping the Emperor as a god. Their focus had shifted away from being willing to die to obey God's commandments. It's ironic, since the Jewish soldiers would have been well acquainted with the sixth commandment, "Thou shalt not kill." Now, they were willing to kill to be able to pick and choose which commandments they wanted to follow. During the war, they were going to have to kill many people, violating the same laws that they wanted to keep.[30]

Even if that sixth commandment applies only to murder, instead of any killing, it would still have forbidden the kinds of wanton slaughter that happened within Jerusalem during the Roman siege of the city. The Zealots, one of the groups in Jerusalem, "Fell upon the population and butchered them like a herd of unclean animals. Ordinary people were killed where they were caught."[31] The Zealots killed about 12,000 of their fellow Jews in this way.[32] After this massacre, the men set their sights on individuals of wealth and power. In one instance, they set up a sham court and put a wealthy man from Jerusalem on trial for made-up crimes.

29. Josephus, *The Jewish War*, 140–1.

30. Ibid., 259–67.

31. Ibid., 260.

32. Ibid., 261.

Though the fake jury found him innocent, two of the Zealots murdered the man in the temple courts anyway. Some of the people of Jerusalem rationalized to themselves that the deaths were necessary to secure their right to obey the Torah without Roman interference. But, in acquiring this freedom, they compromised the very commandments that they were fighting for and secured the destruction of their temple at the hands of the Romans. Here, we see them ignoring God's commands for a different kind of battle and the Israelites suffering the consequences.

This problem with rationalization and disobedience didn't start in Judaism, though. It dates all the way back to Adam and Eve in the garden. We humans have always had a problem with doing what we're told. God said to eat from any of a whole forest of trees, except the one tree that would kill us. But, Adam and Eve thought something like, "Surely we won't die if we eat from this great tree, the God I know wouldn't withhold that from us . . ." He said to eat from any tree but one and yet we could not see the forest he provided because of the one tree from which we were forbidden to eat. Adam and Eve's rationalizations earned them a ticket right out of the garden and into lives of hard work.[33] They forgot that God was protecting them when he told them not to eat the fruit of that tree, not trying to limit or hurt them.

God also wanted to protect Cain when he warned him that he had better change his jealous attitude; that sin was waiting to catch him and take control. But, Cain wouldn't change his attitude and ended up losing control. In his rage, he killed his younger brother and then through his shame, he lied about it to God.[34] Disobedience is in our genes. We cannot seem to help but rationalize our way out of doing what God asks.

Instead of stepping out in faith and doing what God commands, there are those who would rather take matters into their own hands and force others into compliance with God's statutes. We hope that after reading the following chapters on the teachings of Jesus and the Apostles, you will understand more of God's command to be nonviolent. We hope that you will see that the efforts of those who say that war and violence are compatible with Christian doctrine are, in fact, rationalizing just like the Israelites in their encounter with the Canaanites.

In the real war on terror, God requires the same obedience from us as he required from the Hebrew people. With the Cross of Jesus, our heavenly Warrior has declared a new war: a spiritual war, fought with non-violence and with love. Though the orders may seem strange, as they must have to

33. Gen 2:16–17, 3:4–6.
34. Gen 4:7–11.

Jehosaphat's men, we must have faith that God will win the victory. We now struggle with spiritual adversaries to capture the hearts and minds of those held captive by sin and Satan. Through Jesus and Paul, God communicated our battle plans and the rules of engagement. We must obey our noble king, the King of Glory. In later chapters we will outline the new rules of engagement that Jesus and the Apostles gave and offer advice for how we all can obey them.

Peace Treaties

The difficulty for the women mentioned at the beginning of our chapter was that they could not acknowledge that the "God of the Old Testament" is the same God who loves the whole world so much that he took humanity's sins upon himself through his Son, Jesus Christ. Many in the Church today have lost sight of the fact that God's nature has endured throughout the years. "The God of the Old Testament" was the same God who approved of Jesus at his baptism, and he continues to endure, the same, today. From the burning bush, God himself declared, "I am who I am."[35] Even the Psalmist sang out to God, "Your name endures for all generations . . . They (the heavens and earth) will perish, but you endure . . . you are the same, and your years have no end."[36] The same God who ordered the wholesale destruction of Jericho ordered his only Son not to resist his persecutors. "I the Lord do not change."[37] The same God who lashed out ferociously against a fallen world during the time of Noah demands that his followers be models of nonresistance.

So if God never changes, if his nature is the same yesterday today and tomorrow, then what does change? Why does God seem so different in the Old and the New Testaments? We believe that God only changes the way he deals with and reveals himself to humanity. Though he does not change, he does change what we see of him and what he requires of us.

Imagine a mother and a young son in the kitchen. The young boy reaches for the stove and the mother quickly smacks his hand away from the burner, looks her son right in the eye and yells, "NO! HOT! HOT!" Notice that the mother wouldn't sit her small child down at the table and explain to him the dangers of touching a hot burner. The boy is too young to understand such a lesson. He would probably go on to touch the burner anyway and seriously hurt himself.

35. Exod 3:14.
36. Ps 102:12, 102:25–27.
37. Mal 3:6.

Now imagine the mother seeing her 15 year old son reaching for one of his father's beers. Would it be appropriate for her to slap the can out of his hand and yell, "NO! BAD! DRUNK! BAD!"? Of course not, she would do far better to sit her son down and explain to him the dangers of drinking at such a young age. Both her son and the way the mother interacts with him have changed, but the mother has not. Her attitude about his development and her love for him are exactly the same as they were when he was younger, but she must change the ways she teaches him or he will not be able to receive her instruction.

God also changes the way that he relates to us, his children, because we have changed and grown. Just as the small boy was not ready for an articulate, reasonable lesson on kitchen safety, so humanity was not ready for the radical Gospel of the Kingdom of Heaven and its peaceful King, Christ Jesus. God had to prepare humanity for his ultimate teaching, the ultimate revelation of his nature, through his Son.

God chose to deal with his rebellious children, his enemies, in a progressive series of "peace treaties" we Christians call covenants, with each treaty preparing humanity for the next. The first such treaty was with Noah, after God had wiped out every living thing on the face of the planet except Noah, his family and the animals they took with them. Once the flood receded, Noah immediately made a sacrifice to God out of gratitude for his deliverance. When he smelled the fragrance of Noah's grateful sacrifice, God made this declaration of peace toward mankind: "Nor will I ever again destroy every living thing as I have done."[38] As a symbol of his good will, God set his "bow" in the sky for all to see.[39] Every time I see a rainbow, I am reminded of this story of how God began the process of bringing peace to mankind.

A few chapters later, God made another peace treaty with Abraham. Like two tribal chieftains, they barter over the terms and then agree: God will bless the descendents of Abraham and give to him the land of Canaan, and in return Abraham will dedicate himself and his family to God.[40] Abraham moved fast to dedicate his family to God, but God didn't fulfill his promise overnight. It took an awfully long time for the children of Abraham to take over the land of Canaan. There was that little issue of slavery in Egypt. After God used Moses and Aaron to deliver his people

38. Gen 8:21, 9:11.
39. Gen 9:13–14.
40. Gen 15:1–21.

from the hands of Pharaoh, he extended the peace treaty he had made with Abraham by giving the Law to Israel.

It turns out they were (like we are, today) quite adept at not doing what God had said. By the time that Israel split into two nations after the age of the Kings, God's people were regularly breaking the terms of the covenant and going back on the peace treaty that was made by their ancestors. So God raised up nations like Babylon and Assyria against Israel and Judah, because they had begun worshipping other deities, disregarding the poor and oppressed and making treaties with pagan nations. With Babylon in hand, God destroyed Jerusalem and then had the Babylonians, his pagan servants, deport many of his chosen people.[41]

As Jeremiah and some of the other prophets lament over Jerusalem's wasted ruins, a new hope emerges. God promises, "I will restore health to you, and your wounds I will heal."[42] He swears to gather his people back, just as he had scattered them: "Keep your voice from weeping, and your eyes from tears . . . there is hope for your future."[43] All hope had seemed lost: the leaders of God's people were nowhere to be found, the Holy City was lying in ruins, and the temple was burning at the hands of pagan overlords. At this precise moment, God makes a new peace treaty with these indignant people who have turned their backs on the God who graciously saved them from the hand of Pharaoh: "Just as I have watched over them (God's chosen people) to pluck up and break down, to overthrow, to destroy, and to bring evil, so I will watch over them to build and to plant,' says the Lord."[44] "The days are surely coming, says the Lord, when I will make a new covenant with the house of Israel and the house of Judah, it will not be like the covenant that I made with their ancestors."[45] A new pact is to be made. Soon, God will bring peace to his chosen people and radically change how he relates with them and how they relate to him.

Even before the prophet Jeremiah and the fall of Jerusalem, though, the first hints of this new peace treaty had begun to appear in the words of Hosea, Micah, and Isaiah. Writing about 800 years before Jesus walked the streets of Jerusalem, Hosea said that God intended to banish the bow, the sword, and war from the land.[46] Through Hosea, God also promised that

41. Ezek 16 and Jer 25.
42. Jer 30:17.
43. Jer 31:16–17.
44. Jer 31:28.
45. Jer 31:31–32.
46. Hos 2:18.

when he wrote the new covenant, the new peace treaty, he would betroth us to him like a bride to her beloved.[47] God was getting ready to, "have compassion on her who had not obtained compassion," and to, "say to those who were not my people, 'You are my people'"[48]

Hosea's words have come true in the life and death of Jesus. Through Christ's cross, God has shown mercy to all those who have shaken their fist at him and his instructions. He has allowed his salvation to expand beyond Israel to all the nations of the world. The bride has found her groom in Jesus, who paid her bride-price with his death on the cross.[49] We gentiles, who were not God's people, are now part of his chosen people through the death of our Lord, Jesus Christ.[50]

Around Hosea's time, Isaiah and Micah wrote nearly identical passages about this final truce that God was planning to making with humanity. In Isaiah 2 and Micah 4, the prophets described the coming Messiah and how he would shape the world through what he does in Jerusalem. They predicted a new day dawning, with a new kingdom appearing on the horizon. In this new kingdom, the citizens would "beat their swords into plowshares, and their spears into pruning hooks; nation shall not lift up sword against nation, neither shall they learn war any more."[51] To bring peace for his chosen people, God had plans to install a new king in Jerusalem: the anointed one, the Messiah. Micah went on to write that the Messiah would be born in Bethlehem and that he would bring peace to God's people.[52] Both Isaiah and Micah predicted that the Messiah would bring about the day when God's people would no longer fight with earthly, physical weapons.[53]

Since Jesus has paid the price needed for the final peace treaty, the Kingdom of which these prophets wrote has come.[54] The Church is the first fruit of this Kingdom and Jesus is its peace-bearing King: "Peace I leave with you; my peace I give to you; I do not give to you as the world gives."[55] In Luke's record of this moment, Jesus makes it very clear to his

---

47. Hos 2:20.
48. Hos 2:23—*New American Standard.*
49. Matt 9:15.
50. John 1:12; 1 Pet 2:9.
51. Isa 2:4; Mic 4:3.
52. Mic 5:2–5.
53. Mic 5:10.
54. Matt 3:2, 4:17.
55. John 14:27.

disciples that he is passing on the Kingdom of Heaven, as spoken of by the Prophets, to them, "You are those who have stood by me in My trials; and I confer on you, just as My Father has conferred on me, a kingdom, so that you may eat and drink at my table in My kingdom, and you will sit on thrones judging the twelve tribes of Israel."[56]

Through the teachings of his ministry, especially the Beatitudes, Jesus showed us how to do our part under this new peace treaty. We've got to fight God's war on fear with our new weapons, pruning hooks and plowshares. Well, sort of. Christ said that those who came after him would choose to love and not fight. They would lay down their physical weapons and their desire to preserve their own lives at someone else's expense. They would no longer gain what they want or need by taking it by force from someone. Instead, they would make their tools of force and aggression into tools of production. They would produce what they need for themselves and more, so they could share with those who do not have.

We are those who came after Christ. We are the Peaceful Kingdom. The Church today has inherited this tradition of peace from Jesus and the early church. What are we doing with our inheritance? We must turn our swords into plowshares, changing our aggression into production and giving life to the world.

The writings of the Minor Prophets also hint at the coming Kingdom of Heaven. Zechariah, after the destruction of Jerusalem by Babylon, wrote:

> "Rejoice greatly, O daughter Zion! Shout aloud, O daughter Jerusalem! Lo, your king comes to you; triumphant and victorious is he, humble and riding on a donkey, on a colt, the foal of a donkey. He will cut off the chariot from Ephraim and the war-horse from Jerusalem; And the battle-bow shall be cut off, and he shall command peace to the nations . . ."[57]

Zechariah also wrote that the peaceful kingdom to come would be strong in God's spirit, not its own might and power.[58] The Hebrew word translated here as "might," *Chayil*, is more often translated as "army." It is actually the word used to describe Pharoah's army in Exodus 14, but often it is translated as military valor or honor. Essentially, the kingdom to come was not going to be a military power, but a spiritual power. Through Joel, God predicted the day of Pentecost, when the Holy Spirit was poured

56. Luke 22:28–30.
57. Zech 9:9–10.
58. Zech 4:6.

out on all men and women.[59] At Pentecost, Jeremiah's prophecy was also fulfilled as the law was written on the hearts of all men and women, even us non-Jews from the West, Africa, and Asia.[60] Through the cross, the old world has passed away and the peaceful Kingdom of Heaven has appeared on earth.

As we said in the last chapter, God has declared a new war. Christians are soldiers, fighting spiritually for those who do not have life-giving and life-altering faith in Jesus Christ. Though we may be thoroughly physical people, we do not fight physically, as ordinary people fight.[61] In ordinary warfare, insubordination to a superior officer is usually punished with death. Thank God that he doesn't treat us so severely. We were once his enemies, but now he has recruited us into his service through Christ's death.[62] Considering this grace that our king has shown us all, let's join forces with other soldiers of the Kingdom, other followers of Christ. Let's rally around God the warrior and his Son! Let's unite for *his* cause and fight *his* war against fear.

---

59. Joel 2:28–32.
60. Jer 31:33.
61. 2 Cor 10:3–4.
62. Rom 5:10.

3

The Ironic Messiah

"Put your sword back into its place, for all who take the sword shall perish by the sword." Matthew 26:52

WE UNDERSTAND that the Old Testament can be a rather daunting book to read. There are lots of things happening, lot's of metaphors and symbols, and even some poetry. It can be quite difficult to gain practical insight into twenty-first century problems strictly by reading the Hebrew Bible.

Fortunately, God also realized this, and he chose to reveal himself in an even greater way, a way that would leave no questions in anyone's mind. Through this new and complete revelation he could clear up the confusions of the past and pave a righteous yet narrow path into the future. Thus, he gave us his Son, "the image of the invisible God, the firstborn of all creation."[1] By incarnating himself in human form, God was able to reveal himself, communicating his nature and his will to us, his children. Where in the Old Testament God's nature and will for us was shrouded in mystery, now, in the person of Jesus Christ, his will is made known clearly and distinctly: "Long ago God spoke to our ancestors in many and various ways by the prophets, but in these last days he has spoken to us by a Son."[2]

Sometimes we forget that God actually *spoke* to us through Christ. For so many Christians in the world, Christ is just a sacrifice, an unblemished lamb that was slaughtered for the sins of the world. While that is true, we forget that Christ is also God's *revelation*.

Understanding Christ as the answer to the eternal questions "What is God like?" and "What would God have us do?" is the key to overcoming the ethical dilemmas that confuse us. If Christ truly is "the way, the truth,

1. Col 1:15.
2. Heb 1:1.

and the life," then we should be able to gain insight into the will of God by reading about and investigating his life and teachings. Christ's lead can be taken in the face of all these dilemmas. The question of war and violence needs not be any different.

So much is said of having faith in Christ, faith that his sacrifice can cleanse us of our sins. But do we also have faith in his *words?* He is our Savior, but do we acknowledge him as Teacher and Lord as well? Do we seek out his wisdom and his teaching when it comes to orienting our lives? Do we follow his "way"? At first glance most people would probably say "yes," given the WWJD bracelets that our youth wear and all the pictures of Jesus displayed in our churches. But underneath all the lip service we give to the term "disciples of Christ," many Christians in our nation do not believe Christ's commands can be followed or should even be attempted.

Common Sense or *Fallen Sense*

A couple years ago, I (Derek) was serving as a youth pastor in a small, blue-collar church near Akron, Ohio. Fortunately, my wonderful pastor there gave me several opportunities to work with some of the older folks in our church, knowing that it would be a good experience for me before I went off to seminary. On one such occasion, she asked me to teach a mid-week Bible study on the book of Matthew.

The first lesson for the study was the famous Sermon on the Mount, found in Matthew chapters five through seven. We began the study that first night by reading the entire sermon all the way through to ourselves. Once everyone had looked up indicating that they were done, I asked a very simple question: "So what do you guys think?"

"Well . . . it's nice, but he doesn't really expect us to do this stuff does he?"

"What do you mean, George?" I asked.

"I mean, this says we should be perfect as our heavenly Father is perfect, but no one can be perfect, right? And this says that hate is the same as murder! That can't be right. And turning the other cheek is all well and good and everything, but Jesus doesn't want us to be door mats either."

"He doesn't?" I inquired further.

"Well no! He wants us to be strong and defend ourselves. He doesn't want a church full of wimps!" George was getting frustrated.

The truth is that George's frustration is very common in the church today. This aggravation stems from what some call "cognitive dissonance," which occurs when someone holds two conflicting thoughts in their head at the same time and they are unable to resolve the difference between the two ideas. On one hand, we have the teachings of Christ as contained in the Gospels, which say things like, "Turn the other cheek," "Do not resist an evil one but repay evil with good," and "Love your enemies."[3] But on the other hand, we have a church that constantly tells us to revert back to our common sense, to the practical teachings we learned from our parents and our society. Our common sense says that we shouldn't let ourselves be taken advantage of, that sometimes it is necessary to fight fire with fire, and that loving our enemies only works in some far-off, perfect world.

Since our minds can't seem to resolve this issue, most of us simply get frustrated and move on to thinking about other, "more important" matters without ever really dealing with the problem at all. Some academic Christians will take a different course and actually engage the problem head on, trying to harmonize the teachings of Christ with worldly common sense. This is how we end up with pastors giving sermons about how soldiers can love their enemies while killing them, and theologians talking about how Christ gave us these radical teachings only to show us how fallen we truly are by showing us how impossibly holy we would have to be to earn God's favor.

The problem with these kinds of common-sense solutions to George's problem is that they ignore one key point: *common sense is fallen.* Most Christians believe in the fallen-ness of humanity, that through Adam's sin, mankind was plunged into a state of sinfulness that cannot be overcome except by God's grace working through faith in Jesus Christ. However, they don't seem to acknowledge that our *minds* are fallen as well as our flesh. Consider this passage from Paul's first letter to the Corinthians:

> For the message about the cross is foolishness to those who are perishing, but to us who are being saved it is the power of God. For it is written, "I will destroy the wisdom of the wise, and the discernment of the discerning I will thwart." Where is the one who is wise? Where is the scribe? Where is the debater of this age? Has not God made foolish the wisdom of the world?[4]

This passage begs the question, Why are so many in the church today, pastors, theologians, and laity, trying so hard to reconcile the teachings of Christ with the fallen wisdom of the world around us?! Just because the rest of the world believes in something, whether it be revenge or hate or whatever, it does not mean that we have to believe in it too. Actually, the

3. See the Sermon on the Mount, Matt 5: 38–48.
4. 1 Cor 1:18–19.

fact that the world *does* seem to unanimously believe something tells us that we should be wary of it!

Jesus Christ came to turn the whole world and its wisdom upside down. The world tells us that we should all pursue wealth and prosperity, that we should be assertive and strong willed, and that we should avenge the deaths of our countrymen. Jesus, on the other hand, came to proclaim the coming of a Kingdom where the poor would be blessed and where one finds his life by losing it, where the meek inherit the earth and where it is the *peacemakers* who will be called children of God!

With that in mind, let's take a fresh look at the teachings of Christ, not seeking out what our fallen minds want to hear. Instead, let's read with a discerning and humble spirit that is willing to be educated, even if it means transforming our entire worldview. We invite you to join us in taking Paul's advice, "Do not be conformed to this world, but be transformed by the renewing of your minds, so that you may discern what is the will of God—what is good and acceptable and perfect." Let's move on from only believing in the *life and death* of Christ to also believing the life-altering *teachings* of Christ.

The New Law

Before Christ, the watershed event in the history of the people of God was the Exodus, when God, using Moses as his deliverer, led the Israelites out of slavery in Egypt. After God delivered them from their captors, he made a covenant with them, giving them his Law through Moses on Mt. Sinai, that they might form a new nation and live under divine governance. Clearly, the Exodus was *the* defining salvation event for the ancient Israelite religion and continues to be so today.

But God made a change, raising for himself a new "holy nation," using his Son, Jesus Christ as the deliverer. This is evidenced by the constant use of the word "Kingdom" we find in the Gospels, where it is found 114 times. Like the kingdom of Israel, this new Kingdom, which we now call the Church, is defined by a certain standard, a law, if you will, so that we can set an example for the rest of the world. By living in accordance with this second Law, which is merely a fulfillment of the first Law of Moses, we present the solution to the sin problem that has infected humanity. The Church's righteous actions point the way to Christ, who is the solution and antidote for our sick and dying world.

This new Law, this new revelation about how we should live our lives, comes in many places throughout the Gospels, but it is most plainly stated in the "Sermon on the Mount." Here Christ appears on a mountain, much like his predecessor Moses, to give God's commands to his new nation.

The sermon opens with an odd set of blessings (called beatitudes), as Jesus spells out how those who would typically be considered cursed are ironically blessed in the Kingdom of God. Those who are poor in spirit, those who mourn, who are weak, who hunger for righteousness, who are merciful, who are pure in heart, who are peacemakers, and who are persecuted are all considered "blessed" by God.

This small teaching alone calls our violent culture into question. Are those who are merciful on the battlefield blessed in our culture? No, it is those who dominate on the battlefield and take no prisoners who are called our heroes. Are the peacemakers given honor? Sometimes, like with the Nobel Peace Prize, but we mostly admire those folks who succeed in the "fight" for freedom, not those who calm fears and broker peace deals.

The final two "beatitudes" are the most interesting:

> Blessed are those who are persecuted for righteousness' sake, for theirs is the kingdom of heaven. Blessed are you when people revile you and persecute you and utter all kinds of evil against you falsely on my account. Rejoice and be glad, for your reward is great in heaven, for in the same way they persecuted the prophets who were before you.[5]

Does anyone really believe this? Can social or even violent persecution be considered a blessing in our culture? No . . . as Americans, we demand fair and equitable treatment for ourselves at all times. We don't put up with people harassing us because of our beliefs, and we certainly don't tolerate any violence against us! Such a thing demands a swift and violent response right back!

But, if we listen closely enough, the still small voice of Christ is telling us that we should stop defending ourselves, that we should lay down our rights, that we should allow ourselves to be harassed and even killed for the sake of the Gospel . . . that we should even rejoice in our sufferings! In our country we don't rejoice in suffering, we get a lawyer. We're no longer glad to follow in the footsteps of the prophets; instead we opt for security systems, armies, and even guard dogs to safeguard ourselves and our families from our "enemies."

Later in his prolific sermon, Christ speaks on the subject of enemies. He quotes an Old Testament law, already fairly difficult to keep, and takes it to the next level, demanding an even higher level of righteousness:

5. Matt 5:10–12.

> You have heard it was said, "You shall love your neighbor and hate
> your enemy." But I say to you, Love your enemies and pray for those
> who persecute you, so that you may be children of your Father in
> heaven; for he makes his sun rise on the evil and on the good, and
> he sends rain on the righteous and on the unrighteous.[6]

There you have it: the most radical, world changing idea in history.
Nowhere in the world will you find a teaching by a religious leader that
makes less sense or seems more impossible than this, the earth shattering
command to *love* our enemies.

Notice what isn't said here. Christ doesn't say to put up with our
enemies for a time, and then respond with physical or legal violence once
they've pushed us to the breaking point. Christ doesn't say to reserve violence until all diplomatic solutions have been exhausted. Christ doesn't
say to defend yourself and your loved ones. He only says to love your
enemies.

Here we should note the ancient concept of love that Christ had in
mind. The Greek word used by the original author of the Gospel is *agape*,
the strongest form of self-sacrificing love he had a word for. *Agape* is not an
emotion. It is not an inward disposition of the heart. Rather, it is a verb,
an action, something you do. To love someone with *agape* love means that
you have to do something for them, you have to actively love. You have to
seek their benefit and help them wherever you can: "Little children, let us
love, not in word or speech, but in truth and action.[7]"

This is the kind of love with which we are to love our enemies. We are
not just supposed to care about them in some abstract, inward, sentimen-
tal way. We are to love them at our own expense . . . even when we have the
right to hate them. Even after they have wronged us by killing our friends
or relatives, taking advantage of our generosity, robbing us, or even suing
us unjustly, Christ's call to love our enemy persists.

"But that's not fair! We have the right to fight back, to fight fire with
fire. We earned that which we have, so we have a right to defend it!"

Well, the truth is, God doesn't really care about fairness. He makes
this clear in the verses preceding the one about loving your enemies, when
he says,

> You have heard it was said, "An eye for an eye and a tooth for a
> tooth." But I say to you, do not resist an evildoer. But if anyone
> strikes you on the right cheek, turn the other also; and if anyone

6. Matt 5:43–45.
7. 1 John 3:18.

wants to sue you and take your coat, give your cloak as well; and if anyone forces you to go one mile, go also the second mile. Give to everyone who begs from you, and do not refuse anyone who wants to borrow from you.[8]

In our world, if someone slaps you on the face, you have the right to slap back. If someone is going to kill you, you have the right to kill them first. But this kind of self-defense isn't in the teachings of Christ. He says that God makes it to rain on the righteous and the unrighteous alike. He doesn't care about fairness. He doesn't care about you getting what you deserve. (If he did, none of us would be granted salvation, that's for sure!) No, Jesus seeks an end to violence and aggression. He knows that the only way to bring this about is for someone to stop fighting, to lay down their arms even though they might be right, and possibly face unjust death.

Christ goes on to say something striking about his command to turn the other cheek and love enemies:

For if you love those who love you, what reward do you have? Do not even tax collectors do the same? And if you greet only your brothers and sisters, what more are you doing than others? Do not even the gentiles do the same? Be perfect, therefore, as your heavenly Father is perfect.[9]

What Christ is saying here is that he wants his people to *be different*. That was the reason for the first Law that set the Israelites apart from everyone else, and that is the point of this new Law that is supposed to set Christians apart from the pagan world around us. But so many of us don't want to be different. We want to be well-liked. We want to fit in. We want big, well respected churches where everyone is happy and well adjusted. We want to be just like everyone else so that we are never judged for our ridiculous beliefs. So we water those beliefs down to the point that they look just like the common sense beliefs everyone has.

But we have to be different! Our God wants us to stand out, even if it means we're persecuted for our seemingly stupid ideas. After all, he told us that we were blessed when people revile and persecute us, right?

Our world doesn't deal with strange beliefs well. When someone believes something different or more righteous than the world believes, they are often called self-righteous, or judgmental, or even cultic. But that's the price we pay for righteousness, for nonconformity with a faithless world.

8. Matt 5:38–42.
9. Matt 5:46–48.

Those who rely on violence to supply their world with meaning and purpose will, of course, call us cowards and lunatics.

But, we know that Christ was no coward. Even though he was God incarnate, he chose to suffer and die rather than kill those who unjustly murdered him. It was this same Christ who uttered the words "Forgive them Father, for they know not what they do," while he hung on the cross of shame.[10] Was he a coward? Was he a lunatic? Most people think so, and if they think that about him, they'll think the same thing about us: "Servants are not greater than their master. If they persecuted me, they will persecute you."[11]

These teachings are supernatural and they go against our common (yet fallen) sense. This is why Christ later says in this sermon, "Enter through the narrow gate; for the gate is wide and the road is easy that leads to destruction, and there are many who take it. For the gate is narrow and the road is hard that leads to life, and there are few who find it." In a world where Churchgoers are wearing thin the pavement on the wide road, do you have the courage to take the narrow path, the path that requires a radical faith? Do you have the courage to be a pacifist Christian in a world where Christians are known for their violence?

The Disarmed Disciple

There was one notorious Christian who is quite famous for not having the guts necessary for him to be a faithful follower of Christ. On the night Jesus was betrayed by Judas in the Garden of Gethsemane, one disciple (Simon Peter, according to John) decided that he needed to defend his Messiah by force. When the men came to seize Jesus, Peter cut off the ear of one of the soldiers of the high priest. Christ immediately rebuked him for his violence:

> Suddenly, one of those with Jesus put his hand on his sword, drew it and struck the slave of the high priest, cutting off his ear. Then Jesus said to him, "Put your sword back into its place; for all who take the sword will perish by the sword. Do you think that I cannot appeal to my Father, and he will at once send me more than twelve legions of angels?"[12]

Luke goes on to show how after rebuking the disciple, Christ went on to heal the ear of the high priest's soldier, the very man who was coming to

10. Luke 23:34.
11. John 15:20.
12. Matt 26:51–53.

arrest him, "Then one of them struck the slave of the high priest and cut off his right ear. But Jesus said, 'No more of this!' And he touched his ear and healed him."[13]

This short but vivid scene tells much about the character of Christ and about his desire for how we act in the world. Consider Matthew's account, when Jesus tells Peter to put his sword away because all who take the sword shall perish by the sword. Jesus doesn't seem to mean that every soldier will die in the midst of battle, right? I mean, he can't mean that, because we all know that every war has lots of survivors who wield the sword yet do not die. Rather, Christ seems to be saying that the way of the sword only leads to death, that nothing good can come from it. He's telling Peter that the sword is a dead end, and that if he thinks he can extend his life or someone else's by using it, he's wrong. The sword begets the sword; violence only begets more violence.

The ancient Christian Tertullian, who is famous for coining the term "Trinity," put it this way, "Christ, in disarming Peter, disarmed every soldier." You see, Christ's message to Peter was more than just the quiet rebuke of a hot-tempered man. If it had been, then why did all four gospel writers think it important enough to record? Rather, by rebuking Peter at this particular time and in this particular place, Christ is setting a precedent; he is completely changing the rules and making whole the Old Testament teachings on violence. With this new understanding of the scene, Christ's words to Peter, "No more of this!" are not the ramblings of an angry rabbi, but the dramatic declaration of a new age for God's people to look not to the sword for strength, but to the inner faith given to them by God.

Jesus' own life, sinless and perfect, was not worth defending with violence. Think about it this way: Typically when we reveal our belief in Christian nonviolence to our friends and neighbors, they'll invariably come back with a response of something like, "Well, what if someone was trying to kill your wife, or your kids, or your grandma? Would you just let them do it?" Firstly, of course we wouldn't stand idly by while someone tried to hurt our loved ones. We would attempt to put ourselves in between our loved ones and the enemy who might be attacking them, thus taking the hit for them and giving them time to escape.

But we all know that isn't the answer they are looking for. They are wondering if we would use violence to protect our families, if we would hurt or kill the attacker. We point to this passage to answer their question, asking, "If Christ *himself*, is not worthy of a violent defense, then who is? If Christ rebukes Peter for defending his life with the sword, then whose

13. Luke 22:50–51.

life is worth defending? Is an infant's life worth more than the life of God-incarnate? Is your grandma's life worth more than the life of the flawless Lamb of God? Of course not, by saying, "No more of this," Christ wasn't only rebuking Peter for getting in the way of his sacrificial death on the cross, he was laying down an eternal principle, setting an example to be remembered and followed for all of time.

Many theologians cite this very passage as proof that we can't spread Christianity by force in the world. So if we can't defend Christ, if we can't advance *his* cause, *his* Gospel with the sword, then what can we advance with the sword? What ideology is worth so much that we can spread it at the point of a gun, when God himself has told us that we can't use violence to spread Christianity? Is democracy worth more than the Gospel? Is globalization more important than Christ? If we can't fight to spread the faith or defend Christ himself, then we have nothing left to kill for.

The Irony of the Cross

"And what's with all these Christians wearing crosses around their necks?! If Christ ever does come back, you think he's ever going to want to see another (expletive deleted) cross ever again?! That's like going up to Jackie Onasis while wearing a sniper rifle pendant around your neck, saying, 'Hey Jackie, I'm really sorry about your loss.'"[14]

Isn't this true? I mean, I know its profane, but isn't there something shockingly true about what he's saying? Have you ever thought about it before? How can it be that the cross, the instrument of our Savior's gruesome and painful death, can be the most venerated symbol in all of Christianity?! Well, I think we all know that there was something special about that death. Whereas typically humans treat death as a most undesirable event, Christ's death had something special about it . . . something redemptive, something life-giving. Our fear, however, is that Christianity in America has forgotten, or at least dismissed part of that special-ness . . . part of the meaning behind the symbol.

Allow us to explain. If one were to ask a typical, run of the mill, evangelical Christian about the meaning behind the cross, they would probably reply with something that resembles a mathematical formula. Many may even respond with a few select quotes from the book of Romans commonly referred to as the "Romans Road." It usually goes something like this: The first quote is Romans 3:23, "for all have sinned and fall short of the glory of God." This verse is used to make the point that all of humanity

14. Late Comedian Bill Hicks.

is guilty of sin, and is therefore subject to Romans 6:23, "For the wages of sin is death." Here the Christian in question would probably explain that God, due to his infinite goodness, must kill all those who do not perfectly follow his Law. Then they finish out the verse with a bit of hope, "but the free gift of God is eternal life in Christ Jesus our Lord." Then Romans 5:8 is typically quoted, "But God proves his love for us, in that while we were still enemies with God, Christ died for us." At this point the evangelist would typically explain that our sin carries with it a debt of death that must be paid, and since Christ was God incarnate, his death would be the only one sufficient to pay the debt of all humanity. Finally, the "Romans Road" comes to an end with the invitation, "if you confess with your lips that Jesus is Lord and believe in your heart that God raised him from the dead, you will be saved."[15]

There you have it. Theologians call this the theory of penal substitution. Our sin demands our death, but Christ died in our place, and we only need to believe that he did so to be forgiven our debt and be given eternal life. Sounds kind of formulaic, doesn't it? Now we're *not* saying that this is the wrong way to look at Christ's death . . . because it's not. It is very important for Christians to understand that Christ died for us, taking upon himself wrath that was stored up for us because of our unrighteousness. We would like to say, however, that this is not the only meaning of the cross, that Christ's death there should mean a whole lot more to us than just penal substitution.

In our great Christian tradition, the cross has become a symbol for so much more, but in order to understand the meaning behind the cross, we have to take a look at the Christ who hung upon it.

Most Christians would agree that Christ lived a blameless life, that his every character trait should be modeled by Christians. His whole life, however, seems to point to one certain moment, one act of righteousness that would change the course of human history forever: the Cross. In an intimate moment with his twelve disciples, Christ divulges the ultimate meaning of his ministry: "See, we are going up to Jerusalem, and the Son of Man will be handed over to the chief priests and scribes, and they will condemn him to death; then they will hand him over to the Gentiles to be mocked and flogged and crucified; and on the third day he will be raised."[16]

15. Rom 10:9.
16. Matt 20:18–19.

Christ himself went on to explain that the cross would not only be his own destiny, but that it would be the destiny of all of his followers as well:

1. Matthew 10:38—"Whoever does not take up his cross and follow me is not worthy of me."

2. Matthew 16:24, Mark 8:34—"If any want to become my followers, let them deny themselves and take up their cross and follow me."

3. Luke 14:27—"Anyone who does not carry the cross and follow me cannot be my disciple."

Right there are 3 examples of Christ explaining that this death was more than an act of sacrifice which happened long ago and which has little or no bearing on today's life. Why have we forgotten this message? Well, probably because it isn't very popular. Can you imagine a big name evangelist telling a crowd he/she is trying to convert that if they become Christians they will have to suffer, they will have to allow themselves to be mocked, hated and embarrassed, that they will have crucify their pride and selfishness and begin living a life that no longer cares about itself but only about others? Instead, the evangelists of today have taken a lesson from the consumer culture they live in and have reduced the gospel to a "no lose offer." They quote Romans 6:23 that talks of eternal life as a free gift, but they never explain that it is a free gift that will cost you everything you have, "for those who want to save their life will lose it and those who lose their life for my sake will find it."[17]

When will we realize that the Cross, the ultimate act of nonviolence, is meant for us as well? Peter put it this way, "When he was abused, he did not return abuse; when he suffered, he did not threaten; but he entrusted himself to the one who judges justly."[18] Two chapters later he continues, "Since therefore Christ suffered in the flesh, arm yourselves with that same intention (for whoever has suffered in the flesh has finished with sin), so as to live the rest of your earthly life no longer by human desires but by the will of God."[19]

Some people interpret this verse as meaning that we should suffer simply by leading the Christian life. But Christ's suffering was more than an inward frustration over not being able to satisfy his appetites and desires,

17. Mark 8:35.
18. 1 Pet 2:23.
19. 1 Pet 4:1–2.

wasn't it? He suffered a political, unjust death at the hands of those who occupied the seats of power that he rightfully deserved. Even those who came by to watch him be crucified and the criminal on his left taunted him and told him to save himself, since he had so much power as the Son of God.[20]

But he chose not to do it. He chose to die, and then ask God's forgiveness for those who killed him. It's an honor to die as he did. It's Christlike to suffer and die an unjust death, all the while singing God's praises and asking his forgiveness for those who persecute us. Suffering is tough, and human desires constantly lead us away from suffering in the flesh, but if we are going "to arm ourselves with that same intention," we have to be willing to be victims now and then. We will suffer *injustice* that *God's justice* might prevail. It may seem stupid or even nonsensical, but it's the way God chose to redeem humanity.

The False Messiah vs. The Ironic Christ

God's people in Israel had a tough time coming to grips with this ironic Messiah as well. Though they had only been expecting an actual messiah for a few hundred years before Christ's birth, they would never have expected God's Deliverer to look like Jesus of Nazareth.

Almost all theologians agree that the Jews of the first century expected a militaristic messiah. The Israelites had been beaten up for a long time, having been occupied by the Assyrian, Babylonian, Persian and Greek empires. They believed that God had promised them the land of Canaan and that he would drive out any armies who would seek to take their land from them. So when another great empire (Rome) began occupying their territory, they'd had enough.

But they believed very strongly that God would send them a deliverer, a man like Moses who would take hold of the Judean army and government and lead God's people in a revolt against the occupying Roman force. He would secure a stable Holy Land where the Jewish people could live and reign in peace and tranquility. There were more than a few Jews who believed that they were this messiah, but they were all beaten into the ground by Rome's dominant military. So when Christ came, they thought they would finally have their freedom.

This is evident in the stories of Christ's triumphal entry into Jerusalem, where he is seen riding a donkey and being greeted as a king by his fellow Jews waving palm fronds. But a few days later the story would be very dif-

20. Matt 27:38–44.

ferent as Christ would be taken into the custody of the Roman Procurator Pontius Pilate. It became obvious to them that this was not the messiah they were looking for; this is not the messiah who would stain the roads of Jerusalem red with the blood of gentiles and secure an era of peace and safety for God's people.

The same crowd that welcomed Jesus to Jerusalem because they believed he would set them free from pagan occupation now hurled curses at him and pleaded with Pilate to kill him:

> Then they all shouted out together, "Away with this fellow! Release Barabbas for us!" (This was a man who had been put in prison for an insurrection that had taken place in the city, and for murder.) Pilate, wanting to release Jesus addressed them again; but they kept shouting, "Crucify, crucify him!"[21]

After it was painfully obvious for them that this weak and bloody Christ was not the christ they were looking for, they had no more use for him. The Christ they once welcomed as their king on a donkey, they now wished to kill on a cross. Also, notice the man they wanted released instead of Jesus. Barabbas was a revolutionary and a zealot, someone who tried to bring about Israelite freedom by force. Now this is someone the first-century Jews could get behind! Someone who gets things done, who takes the bull by the horns and kills his enemies! So he is released and the pacifist, nonviolent revolutionary is nailed upon a cross and left to die.

We believe that many in American Christianity have called for this same switch. Instead of accepting the nonviolent Messiah we have been given, they have exchanged him for a militaristic christ who uses the sword to establish justice. They think that if Christians take control of the government and military, we can build God's Kingdom in the world. They really believe that if they could only get enough votes and enough guns, the world could be made Christian.

This is idol-worship. God didn't give us a militaristic messiah; to pretend that he did is to worship someone other than the only begotten Son of God. When will the church embrace the Messiah we *have* been given, the Messiah who doesn't make sense and can't be defended by the sword. When will we accept the Messiah who chooses not to call down twelve legions of angels, and opts instead to die an unjust death? When will we be true *Christ*ians, followers of the true Christ?

---

21. Luke 23:18–21.

The Victory of Victimhood

Have you ever been to an Orthodox Christian church? It's quite stunning. The sanctuary is typically lit with candles and light coming in from huge, beautifully colored stained glass windows. The bright, colorful beams of sunlight can be seen as they pass through little foggy clouds of incense. There are hand-painted icons everywhere, depicting Christ, Mary, and other heroes of the faith. At the front is the altar, where everything is made of gold and glistens in the sunlight. At the center of all of this pomp-and-circumstance is the Crucifix, a bigger than life-size sculpture of the beaten and broken body of Christ hanging from the old wooden beams of the cross . . . how ironic!

It is fortunate that we have Orthodox churches and beautiful Roman Cathedrals to show us the glory of the Cross. We need to be reminded of the victory of *victimhood*. You see, the Cross is a symbol. It symbolizes the death of a man who wouldn't be weighed down by his own fears, a man who chose not to fight back, a man who obeyed God's call to death rather than defending himself. Those who would like to use Christianity for their own gain and who would like all the benefits of the cross without being willing to bear it themselves, have reduced our beloved symbol to a mathematical formula. To them it's a "no lose offer", a far off event that happened long ago so we can all be happy and live our best lives now. But they don't understand the cross that all of us are called to bear. When are the Christians of the world going to start looking like Christ? When will they realize that Christ's nonviolence was meant to be a model, a proto-type of our own nonviolence? Will the Church ever have the "prayer in the garden experience" and come to grips with the ridiculousness of God's commands? Will we ever start fighting the *real* war on terror?

4

A Tradition of Peace

"But they have conquered (the Dragon) by the blood of the lamb and by the word of their testimony, for they did not cling to life even in the face of death." Revelation 12:11

A s WE said in the first chapter, our struggle with violence and non-violence led us to Scripture. We have attempted, in these last two chapters, to present what we found in the Hebrew Scriptures, the words of Christ, and the work of Christ. With this chapter, we will move on to the history of nonviolence in Church tradition. We contend that from the time of the Apostles down to today, at least one part of the Church has rejected violence for the sake of their conscience.[1] Sometimes that part was the majority of Christians. Unfortunately, though, it has typically been the minority. With this chapter we hope to pick up on the trail left by all of these nonviolent peacemakers and learn what we may from their legacy.

We think it is very important to learn from these folks who went before us because we believe that their journeys were all parts of the story of God. Although the Bible has the highest authority for us Christians today, the experiences and thoughts of the Christians of ages past must also be considered. We believe that the story didn't end when the Apostle John penned the last words of the book of Revelation, but that God has been continuously speaking to and leading his people since that day.

We aren't sure that the Christians who came before us were always listening to God. At times, they were listening to the pagan world in which they lived or the fear in their own hearts. Between you and us, Derek and Jon aren't perfect at listening to God's voice over the cloud of voices that surrounds around us, either. Sometimes, at least, God's people get it wrong. Because of this, we have to be careful when studying the history of Christianity to make sure that we don't place that history over Scripture. Tradition and Holy Scripture should form one cohesive body of

1. 1 Pet 2:19–20.

truth. Since Scripture is unchanging, it is the authoritative basis we must use to distinguish "good tradition" from "bad tradition." Nonetheless, we can still hear God calling to us through the stories of the brave men and women who bore the name and banner of Christ before us.

When studying and reading about the people of the early Church, we must also consider that they weren't thinking in the ways that Western society has taught us to think. For instance, we here in America are taught to fear death above all else. Many of our news shows, dramas and horror movies are all about how terrible death is and how it is to be avoided at all costs. They did not fear death, as we here in Western society do. They lived and breathed Christ's teaching, "Do not fear those who kill the body but are unable to kill the soul; but rather fear Him who is able to destroy both soul and body in hell."[2] The faith of the early Christians and the work of the Holy Spirit gave them a confidence that could not be shaken by the threat of death, no matter how or when that threat came. Literally, death had no sting for early Christians.[3] In fact, the evidence seems to indicate that the early Church (and many Christians since then) viewed death as victory. This is the exact opposite of our society's values, which teach us to preserve our life and the lives of those around us at almost any cost.

Many sources lead us to this conclusion about early Christians. The first of these is the New Testament Scriptures. To the elders of the Ephesian Church, Paul preached, "But I do not count my life of any value to myself, if only I may finish my course and the ministry that I received from the Lord Jesus."[4] To the Philippian Christians, he wrote, "For to me, living is Christ and dying is gain."[5] Everything Paul did was with the single purpose of serving Christ. To that end, he was willing to give God the choice to end his life as *God* saw fit. If God let him live, it was only so that he could work more for the advance of the Gospel. If God allowed him to die, he was in Heaven with Jesus and had won victory over death.

The way that the early Church recorded martyrdoms also reveals this unusual attitude toward death. In *The History of the Church*, the bishop Eusebius frequently refers to martyrs as finding "glorious fulfillment"[6] or winning the "prize of an end like that suffered by the Lord."[7] Eusebius

2. Matt 10:28.

3. 1 Cor 15:55; Ps 23:4.

4. Acts 20:24.

5. Phil 1:21.

6. Eusebius, *The History of the Church*, 123; 268.

7. Ibid., 95.

likely witnessed and heard of hundreds or thousands of "victories won by devoted martyrs all over the world."[8] Since he lived during many of these fierce, bloody persecutions, his opinion on martyrdom is worth looking at. From his accounts, we can better understand the early Christian community's attitude toward martyrdom.

Consider also the book of Revelation, written almost entirely to encourage the early Church to die rather than sacrifice incense at the altar of the Emperor Domition who was requiring the worship of his subjects. "They did not cling to life even in the face of death."[9] John wanted persecuted Christians to know that their lives were a gift from God in the first place, God's to give and take as he pleased. This understanding was to give them the courage to be nonviolent, even when facing their deaths.

Peter was also encouraging the suffering Church when he wrote, "Since therefore Christ suffered in the flesh, arm yourselves also with the same intention (for whoever has suffered in the flesh has finished with sin), so as to live for the rest of your earthly life no longer by human desires, but by the will of God."[10] While the world around them sought to terrorize the hearts of Christians by hunting and killing them, Peter reassured them that their fate would be the same as their Master's, and that by walking in his footsteps, they could blot out all that separated them from God.

Another resource that tells us about the early Church's attitudes is a book called the *Didache*, or "the teaching." Tradition tells us that the twelve Apostles wrote it as a training manual for new believers, to be memorized in preparation for baptism. In one section of the *Didache*, a good man and an evil man are contrasted. Evil men were described as, "those not showing mercy to the poor," and, "not toiling for the one weighed down by toil."[11] Christ's followers are to be selfless workers, but the evil man is selfish, refusing to lift a finger to help those who are in need. For, "We know love by this, that He laid down His life for us; and we ought to lay down our lives for one another. How does God's love abide in anyone who has the world's goods and sees a brother or sister in need and yet refuses help?"[12]

The Apostles taught these new Christians to help the needy, but also to become longsuffering, merciful, and harmless.[13] Helping those in need

8. Ibid., 268.

9. Rev 12:11.

10. 1 Pet 4:1.

11. Milevic, *The Didache: Text, Translation, Analysis, and Commentary*, 5:2.

12. 1 John 3:16–17.

13. Milevic, *The Didache: Text, Translation, Analysis, and Commentary*, 3:8.

doesn't require a willingness to stick to a cause, "at any cost." A Christian can respond to poverty and injustice righteously while still respecting the sanctity of *all* life, the oppressor and the oppressed. With meekness and gentleness, these early Christians labored for the afflicted. They often gave their lives, but would not take the life of another. That was one price they could not afford, and neither can we.

Many folks today would see violence as a justified response when the weak are being oppressed by the strong. We are taught that there is no higher virtue than to defend the weak, with violence when necessary. But Jesus never taught that and neither did the Apostles. To Jesus, the highest virtue, the highest love, is not to defend our friends with violence, *but to lay down our lives for our friends*.[14] The perfect love of Jesus had no enemies, only friends. That is why God chose to make peace with us through Christ. His perfect love saw no enemies, only friends who had become separated from him. To Christ, his own life was worth less than the price of making peace. When we consider our lives worth less than even our enemies' lives, that is the perfection of love. That is the kind of love that the early Church thought was required of all Christians. Can we find the courage to have no enemies, only separated friends?

But, how is this possible? Refusing to use violence would mean that we wouldn't be perfectly effective in our defense of the weak and afflicted. Surely the protection of life is worth the lives of a few violent bullies and tyrants! Well, we were certainly taught by our culture that this is true. But that is not the message of Scripture or the message that was given to the early Church. Take, for instance, the third chapter of the letter to the Romans. Paul spends the first eight verses making a case that he would *never* say that Christians should do evil in the course of bringing about good. "By no means!" he says.[15] Later, he wrote "Never pay back evil for evil to anyone."[16] Evil, oppression, and injustice were not, and are not, valid excuses for Christians to kill anyone. Christians are supposed to conquer evil with good, not with more evil.[17]

More than one hundred years after Paul, Tertullian wrote this on the ethical problem of using violence to overcome evil, "If we are enjoined, then, to love our enemies, as I have remarked above, whom have we to

14. John 15:13.
15. Rom 3:6.
16. Rom 12:17.
17. Rom 12:21.

hate? If injured, we are forbidden to retaliate, lest we become as bad ourselves: who can suffer injury at our hands?"[18]

Another early Christian writer, Origen, lived in the generation immediately following Tertullian. Though Origen wrote close to two hundred years after Jesus lived, he seems to have seen eye to eye with Paul and Tertullian on the issue of violence. He argued that since Jesus did not approve of violence because he never tolerated it amongst his disciples, only rebuked it.[19] Unlike the Jewish faith from which Christians are descended, Christians could not use violence to accomplish their goals. Origen also records that in the Christian community, they had "adopted laws of so exceedingly mild a character as not to allow them, when it was their fate to be slain as sheep, on any occasion to resist their persecutors."[20]

From the writings of these men we can see that the early Church was taught the nonviolence of Jesus' teachings. Perhaps the clearest example of this message to the early Church comes from Hippolytus of Rome's *Apostolic Tradition*. Hippolytus, a theologian from around 200 AD, wrote many works of theology. However, we are most interested in a section of the *Apostolic Tradition* where he lists the occupations that Christians were not allowed to hold. Certain jobs that we would expect appear in the list, like pimps, pagan priests, astrologers, and prostitutes. Gladiators, charioteers, and those who were involved in the production of those events were also not allowed membership in the Church unless they found other jobs.[21]

Additionally, local politicians and military governors, with "the authority of swords," were not allowed in the Church unless they resigned their posts.[22] Both of these positions would have allowed, perhaps even expected, the officials to sometimes punish people with death.[23] If a Christian was already in the military, he had to refuse to execute anyone. Based on this, we believe that the authority to punish with death was the exact reason that they were not allowed in the Church. This ban on violence was so strict that if a Christian who was already a member of the Church joined the army, he was no longer allowed in the community.[24]

18. Tertullian, "Apology," 42.

19. John 18:10–11.

20 Origen, "Against Celsus," 48.

21. Hippolytus, *On the Apostolic Tradition*, 100.

22. Ibid., 100.

23. Ibid., 102.

24. Ibid., 100.

When the Church was in its youngest, most pure state, less than 200 years from the resurrection of Christ, we can clearly see that the use of violence was not tolerated among God's people.

The Christians who refused to use the tool of violence have not always been successful, by the world's standard. For example, during the persecutions under the Roman emperors, nonviolence cost the lives of many Christians. Sadly, sometimes Christians even died at the hands of other people who called themselves followers of Christ. In the 16th Century, tens of thousands of Anabaptists were killed at the hands of governments with the support of both Catholic and Protestant Christians. They were killed, but their faith survived them in the many modern churches deriving their roots from the Anabaptist movement, including the Brethren, Amish, Friends, and Mennonite Churches.

From these churches was born a group called CPT, Christian Peacemaker Teams. CPT is multi-denominational group that focuses their efforts on "getting in the way" of injustice, all around the world. They give voices to the helpless and offer themselves and their service, nonviolently, to help prevent atrocities in war-torn areas like Israel and Palestine, Rwanda and the Sudan, Eastern Europe, and even Cleveland, Ohio! To the non-Christian world, this is all utter foolishness. But, although their lives may be taken, they know that they gain eternal life through Christ, in Heaven.

Over the centuries, there have been many millions of Christians who have died faithfully, when turning the other cheek to their persecutors. However, there have also been many successes won through nonviolent means. In the early 1900's, Russian peasants held labor strikes to protest the injustices of the Tsar and those in power in Russia. They were, in part, influenced by Christian writer Leo Tolstoy's writings on nonviolent resistance and non-cooperation with unjust governments. Though it took eighty years and they resisted two different corrupt governments, the nonviolent work that they started eventually defeated both the Tsar and Russian communism![25]

The early successes of those nonviolent peasant strikers impressed one young lawyer in South Africa. He took note of how they had ended injustice without using the sword. One year later, this same man watched as the South African government increased their discrimination against people from India, his homeland. Leaving a lackluster legal career, he helped to lead a movement against this inequality. Over the next 25 years,

25. Ackerman and Duvall, *A Force More Powerful: A Century of Non-Violent Conflict*, 25–30, 57–8.

he returned to India and led a group of nonviolent men and women resisting British imperial rule, with sit-ins, hunger strikes, and a protest march across the poor countryside to raise awareness of the inequality of the imperial system. Because of his nonviolent success against the British, Gandhi has become a household name.[26]

Gandhi's work, along with Christ's teachings and the influence of the Holy Spirit, encouraged leaders in the American Civil Rights movement like Rev. James Lawson and Dr. Martin Luther King, Jr. to pursue equality with nonviolence.[27] Take a look at some of Rev. Lawson's list of dos and donts for participants in the nonviolent sit-ins: "1. (Do not) strike back nor curse if abused . . . 4. (Do) refer information seekers to your leader in a polite manner . . . 5. (Do) remember the teachings of Jesus Christ, Mahatma Gandhi, and Martin Luther King. Love and nonviolence is the way."[28] These two men initiated change as the Apostles did, by giving their lives to their cause. As they waged war on the fear that was being heaped on their people, they successfully stayed true to Jesus' prohibition of violence for his disciples.

The evils of racism in the American South and in India were causes worth fighting against with nonviolence. But, when we discuss the ideals of nonviolence with others, we are asked far more commonly about World War II and Hitler than any other social or political issue. Would a position of nonviolence require Christians to stay home against such a force of evil as Nazi Germany? Absolutely not! The greater the evil, the greater the need for nonviolent action against it. To end our look at the narrative of Church tradition and Christian nonviolence, we would like to tell a brief story about the Danish resistance to the Nazis in the 1940's.

Denmark fell to Germany in April 1940. At that time, the Nazis had not yet begun the methodical slaughter of Jews, gypsies, and the infirm. Some Danes greeted the occupiers with warmth, but one teenager couldn't bring himself to be happy with occupation. When Arne Sejr saw a newspaper article urging him, and his people, to behave like "good Danes," he wasn't sure what they meant. He struggled with the idea at first, but then began to form a clear vision of the "Good Dane." His manifesto, "Ten Commandments for Danes," urged his fellow citizens to find and use ways to passively resist their invaders. They destroyed machinery, worked

26. Ibid., 62–109.

27. Ibid., 307–8.

28. Ibid., 321.

poorly or refused to work for the Germans, and otherwise caused a general ruckus.[29]

When the Nazis tried to round up all of the Jews of Denmark, the Danish Christians not only warned them, but also hid them in their own homes and apartments to protect them from the Nazi soldiers. The Nazis then pressed the issue and the Danes smuggled their Jewish neighbors to safety in Sweden on any and every available boat, listing their cargo as sacks of potatoes to avoid suspicion. When the dust settled, the Germans had only captured 472 Jews. 7,220 Danish Jews had been saved from the awful fate that would have awaited them in German concentration camps.[30] The people of Denmark managed to hold off Nazi domination for the entire course of the war, mostly through nonviolent means.[31]

It should be noted that we do not tell their stories because we think that nonviolence will always be victorious, in the way the world sees victory. We tell their stories because, like Mother Teresa, Martin Luther King, and the Christians of CPT, they have chosen to fight evil without using more evil themselves. All of these people saw the peace of God as the presence of unity, equality and truth, not the absence of conflict. As they labored for their brothers and sisters, they chose to be faithful to the nonviolence that Jesus commanded on the mount, though it sometimes hurt. Though they knew that they might not see the fruit of their labors, they were willing to be faithful in their small part of the struggle. We see these people as heroes and role models for the people of the Church, second only to Christ.

Personally, I must note that it is tempting to leave the story here and move on to the next section of the book. It would be much easier if I could tell you that the Church has always been a force for good in the world and abstained from violence, as we believe Jesus commanded us to. However, about three hundred years after Jesus lived, a dissenting viewpoint on violence began to grow in popularity. Christianity had been in a struggle for its own existence against the armies of Rome. It had existed as a counter-cultural force, holding its position against all things unholy, including the culture and emperors of Rome. In this struggle, Christians were regularly forced to rely on the will, power, and Spirit of God as their only defense.

With the rise of Constantine, the first "Christian" emperor of Rome, that all changed. Now, the Church had become the super-culture in the Mediterranean. Constantine endorsed Christianity as the official religion

29. Ibid., 211–2, 218, 220–3.
30. Ibid., 223–4.
31. Ibid., 230.

of the Roman Empire and endowed the Church with some of his land and imperial wealth.[32] With this shift in power came a major change in the Church's perception of strength. Jesus taught complete reliance on God's strength and providence, but this teaching was now obsolete and passé to a Church that was marrying herself to Rome. Though Christians had previously needed God to protect them and sustain them, they now had a "Christian" emperor to do that. Christians began to participate in the military more often. The goals of the Church could now be accomplished primarily through human effort and ingenuity. They only needed God to take care of what happened after death.

This change is directly related to the study of nonviolence because less than one hundred years after the Christianization of the Roman Empire, this different view on violence had been formulated, recorded, and accepted by the Church. Over the centuries, this new perspective on the use of violence by Christians came to be known as *Just War Theory*. Basically, Just War Theory proposes that for a Christian to be able to participate in and support a war, it must meet certain criteria. First, this kind of war may only be fought as a last resort. Second, a proper authority, such as a king or government, must authorize the war. Third, the intention of the violence must be to bring about justice, such as protecting the weak or getting revenge for a wrong suffered. Also, the violence used may only be in reasonable proportion to the original violence suffered (there are several rules applying to this one).[33]

Many Christians agree with this position, because it is more comfortable and it is the official position of several large Christian denominations (and non-denominational independent churches). Many Christian theologians have contributed to this theory over the centuries, including St. Augustine and St. Thomas Aquinas. A number of governments have claimed to use its principles to guide their foreign policy and direct their armies. However, it is not widely publicized that this theory has its roots in pre-Christian Roman religion. Rarely is it told that for several hundred years before Christ's birth, there was a group of pagan Roman priests (called *fetiales*) whose responsibility it was to tell the Roman government when and how it could fight wars, in much the same way that Christian

---

32. For more on this, check out the section on Constantine in *The Story of Christianity*, by Justo Gonzalez. (Harper Collins, 1984).

33. See Brian Orend's *The Morality of War* page 15 or google "Just War Theory" for more info on these principles.

religious leaders used Just War Theory to tell their friends in the government when and how to fight wars.[34]

Historians tell us that this group may have survived until at least the time of the emperor Augustus (27 BC to 14 AD).[35] This would have been around the time that Jesus was born, and just after a Roman politician, Marcus Tullius Cicero, wrote an essay called *Just War* which described the moral guidelines with which Rome should fight her wars. This all happened three or four hundred years before Augustine started writing his Just War Theory for Christians. In other words, the whole thing is named after an essay on ethics by a non-Christian.

When comparing the two, one can't help but notice the similarities between the principles of Just War Theory and Cicero's essay. For instance, Just War Theory requires that a legitimate authority, like a legislative body or king, must declare the war for it to be considered a "just war."[36] This principle is basically identical to Cicero's, "No war is considered just unless it has been proclaimed and declared, or unless reparation has first been demanded."[37]

Consider also the principle on self-defense. One of the main justifications for going to war, according to Just War Theory, is self-defense. When a country is attacked, it is considered "just" for the country to retaliate and redress the wrong that was suffered."[38] Compare this to Cicero's: "A war is never undertaken by the ideal state, except in defense of its honor or its safety." He goes on, "Those wars are unjust which are undertaken without provocation. For only a war waged for revenge or defense can actually be just."[39] But Jesus specifically prohibited his disciples from taking revenge![40] Just War Theory apparently takes Cicero as its moral guide more than the teachings of Jesus! But we, as Christians, must weigh Jesus' moral authority above Cicero's. Cicero was a fair man and a just thinker. However, Cicero was not our Messiah, the very image of the invisible God.

How can we expect Christians who serve as soldiers to exact revenge on behalf of the country in which they live and also love their enemies, the very men that they fight? If we are allowed or even expected to fight

---

34. Dumezil, *Archaic Roman Religion*, 123.

35. Hornblower and Spawforth, *Oxford Classical Dictionary*, 594.

36. Orend, *The Morality of War*, 32, 40.

37. Cicero, "De Republica," 25.

38. Orend, *The Morality of War*, 32, 40.

39. Cicero, "De Republica," 25.

40. Matt 5:39, 44.

to defend ourselves and our country, how can also we love our enemies by bearing all things, enduring all things, or not taking into account a wrong suffered?[41]

Even if Christians simply guided their warfare by the rules of Just War Theory, there would be a major change in military strategy. First, we'd have to eliminate pre-emptive strikes as violations of the last resort principle. Second, all military action, including CIA operations and secret strikes, would require prior approval of one of America's legislative bodies. Is it likely that our generals would agree to have all their battle strategies reviewed and approved by our politicians? Third, all violence would need to account for protecting the weak and achieving justice. So, each soldier would need to be accountable for eliminating civilian casualties. In the heat of battle, Christians would need to wait until they could determine that each bomb they dropped and each shot they fired would not harm non-combatants.

A theologian at Duke University, Stanley Hauerwas, asked when reflecting on these same issues, "Could you really trust a person in your unit who thinks the enemy's life is as valid as his own or his fellow soldier's? Could you trust someone who would think it more important to die than to kill unjustly?"[42] It is pretty clear that America's military isn't set up to handle the strict requirements of Just War Theory. It doesn't seem likely that those who are in power in our military would be likely to want to change everything so that they could comply, either. Looking over the history of warfare, there aren't many wars that have met these requirements. Frankly, we haven't yet come across one war in which either side fought in complete compliance with Just War Theory. There are too many human parties involved for that to ever happen. As we have noted before, we just don't do well when entrusted to give vengeance with our own hands.

Perhaps that is why the early Church completely outlawed violence by its members. We believe that they refused violence because they could see no connection between truly loving God and hating anyone.[43] For them, there was no greater love of enemies than to give up their own lives for the lives of their enemies. Since they could not and would not kill their enemies, who was left to kill? They fought the war on terror by refusing to take up arms as an expression of their love of God and of neighbor. We pray that we can have that same devotion.

41. Matt 5:44; 1 Cor 13:4–8.

42. Hauerwas *Dispatches from the front: Theological Engagements with the Secular*, 154–5.

43. 1 John 4:8, 4:12, 4:20–21.

5

The Inner Struggle

"Fight the good fight of the faith; take hold of the eternal life, to which you were called and for which you made the good confession in the presence of many witnesses." 1 Timothy 6:12

IN ORDER for this work to mean anything, in order for this book to have any impact on Christians at all, this all-important question must be answered: "So . . . how should we live?" If everything we have just said is true, how should we as Christians live our daily lives? Practically speaking, what distinguishes a nonviolent Christian from everyone else? Christian nonviolence is a vain, meaningless philosophy if it has nothing to say to everyday Christians about how they go about their daily business.

Firstly, it has helpful to distinguish between the two fronts in the Christian war: the inner (personal) front, where the believer does battle with his own sinful appetites and desires, and the outer (social) front, where the believer confronts the evil found in the social world around her. Much like the authentic Islamic concept of Jihad, the true Christian struggle is fought both within and outside the body, an inner and outer struggle.

The Inner Struggle

The Inner Struggle is the battle against the sin within oneself. Sin is defined by different people in many different ways. Unfortunately, there is no way that we could offer a definition of sin that would satisfy everyone, but for our purposes, we will define sin as that part of ourselves that rebels against God's love and plan for his creatures. Sin is the force that compels us to seek our own good, forsaking the good of others and the good that God knows will benefit us.

As we mentioned above, we feel that the decisive blow in the struggle against sin and terror has already been struck by Christ's death and resurrection. His Church, however, must carry on his struggle, warring as he did against the demonic forces of evil still devouring the lives and souls of the people in our midst. Therefore, it is our duty as Christians to carry on this struggle, first by purifying ourselves of the poison of sin. Once that process has been started, we must begin working to introducing others to the lifesaving antidote, faith in Christ Jesus. So our fight continues.

A great example of a poorly fought battle against sin is the story of Cain and Abel. Cain, the older brother, apparently works less hard preparing his sacrifice to the LORD than does his younger brother Abel. When God refuses to accept Cain's offering, jealousy and anger toward his brother begin to swell within Cain. God, sensing this, warns Cain, "Sin is lurking at the door; its desire is for you, but you must master it."[1] Cain does not heed the Father's warning, and sin soon overtakes him as he carefully plans and carries out his brother's murder.

What could Cain have done differently? Well, God told him that he must "master" his sin. Sin is a given here. Sin lies within every one of us. We may not be able to purge ourselves completely of this foreign evil, but we can master it, take control of it, and not allow it to rule our lives. Had Cain mastered the sin that caused him to kill his brother, he could have turned his initial anger into motivation to work harder in preparing his sacrifice. God seems to say this in Genesis 4:6–7: "Why are you angry, and why has your countenance fallen? If you do well, will you not be accepted?" God didn't have it in for Cain, he truly wanted Cain to succeed. He wanted him to turn his anger into love, faith, and motivation. Anger is an essentially destructive force in our lives, but if mastered, it can be turned into a creative force.

Christians today are in a very similar situation as Cain. We constantly fall short in our offerings to God. We are told that we are to be holy and living sacrifices to the Father, a feat we fail at nearly every day.[2] But every time we fail before God or even one another, we become angry. Choosing not to be angry at ourselves, we often displace our anger onto others, and feelings of jealousy and resentment begin to cloud our thoughts. Before we know it, we are having fantasies about conflicts, some of which are violent. But in his Sermon on the Mount Christ tells us, "You have heard that it was said to those of ancient times, 'You shall not murder'; and 'whoever

---

1. Gen 4:7.
2. Romans 12:1.

murders shall be liable to judgment.' But I say to you that if you are angry with a brother or sister, you will be liable to judgment."[3]

So you see, killing someone and wanting to kill them is the same offense to God. Often, the threat of capital punishment or imprisonment is the only thing stopping someone who has developed the desire to kill. God wants his people to live under his rule not because they are forced to, or because someone might kill them if they don't, but out of love for God and his creation. We shouldn't want to murder because we know God loves whoever it is we hate. How can we hate that which the Creator-God of the Universe loves?

So you see, Cain was guilty of murder the moment he let his anger overtake him. The violence he lashed out with against Abel was only a product of the sin that had run amok in his soul. The sin wasn't the violence itself; the sin was the heart-condition that led to the violence. Violence was an outward projection of an inward disposition. Violence is the symptom; the sin of hate is the disease.

We Christians must be ever vigilant over our own emotions. We must "take every thought captive to obey Christ."[4] Violence begins in the heart; therefore, nonviolence must start in the heart as well. The struggle against violence is a struggle against our own animal instincts. It is natural for us to be angry and to hold grudges against those who wrong us. It is natural to displace our hatred of ourselves onto others. These are ordinary reactions. But Christianity recognizes the fallen-ness of the world and therefore the fallen-ness of the ordinary. Violence is a natural part our existence, but it is a natural part of existence outside of love. When we live outside the grace and love of God violence becomes an accepted, even necessary, part of life. But once we have gained the divine perspective, once we truly understand God's love for us and the rest of his creation, it becomes overwhelmingly apparent that violence cannot be a part of the Kingdom of God, and that it has no place among his people.

Unlike Cain, Jesus had mastery over anger and did not fall victim to sin. As Christ was nailed to the cross, suffocating and bleeding from the wounds he received at the hands of Pilate's soldiers, he turned to those who were mocking them, looked toward heaven and said, "Father, forgive them; for they do not know what they are doing."[5]

3. Matt 5:21–22.

4. 1 Cor 10:5.

5. Luke 23:34.

Christ led a sinless life, never doing harm to anyone. He had committed no crime and was spotless before God. He did not deserve to die, and he knew it. He could have called down the heavenly host to come and destroy all of his persecutors, and he could have instantly annihilated Judas, Pilate, and Herod. But he didn't. He didn't allow himself to feel anger against those who betrayed him. Instead, he chose to look at them with God's eyes, with God's love, and when he did that, he didn't see malicious, blood-thirsty men and women; he saw poor, confused children that didn't even realize they were hurting a Father who loved them.

As Christians, we must try to find Jesus' perspective. Many will hurt us. This is undeniable and unavoidable. However, we must see those who would do us harm not as violent agents of evil, but as lost children of God who have not yet allowed themselves to feel God's touch of love and grace. It is impossible to communicate God's message of redemption to lost souls while acting violently against them. Jesus knew that he could show his captors God's love only by allowing himself to be hurt, by taking their punishment, rather than responding in anger. Jesus knew that it was better to allow himself to be killed rather than fighting back and thus closing the ears of his executioners.

Another good example of fighting the Inner Struggle is found in Paul's first letter to the Corinthian church. It appears that believers are quarreling with one another and are taking their cases to a pagan, secular court to be decided.[6] Upon hearing this, Paul is extremely upset that Christians would allow their disputes to be settled by those outside the Kingdom, outside the Church. He doesn't understand why they would put their destinies in the hands of pagans, who know nothing of God's teaching and who enforce their decisions and statutes with violence. Furthermore, Paul asks, "In fact, to have lawsuits at all with one another is already a defeat for you. Why not rather be wronged? Why not rather be defrauded?"[7]

Paul's words are absolute rubbish to the unbelieving world. We in America believe that we have a right to live our lives free from wrongdoing, and that if someone does trespass against us, we have a right seek restitution, even vengeance. But both Paul and Christ bid us to a higher call. Both remind us that we already have all we could ever want in Christ's inheritance, and that we need not worry about being wronged here on earth, because whatever suffering we endure here on earth will only be

6. 1 Cor 6:1–8.
7. 1 Cor 6:7.

temporary.[8] It is better to allow ourselves to be hurt and leave our enemies asking, "Wow, why don't they fight back? What is it that they believe in? Why don't they want vengeance?" We can know that suffering for the Kingdom in this way is actually a wonderful privilege.[9]

But this is a very tall order. Christ did an amazing thing by praying for his enemies while he was on the cross. Allowing ourselves to be wronged in this way goes against everything that has been taught to us. It goes against both nature and nurture. During our years on earth, the "elemental spirits of the universe" get lots of opportunities to fill our heads with images and messages that often find themselves at odds with the Gospel of peace and reconciliation. We see movies and television shows about soldiers, cops and vigilantes who righteously inflict judgment and condemnation on those whom they perceive as evil-doers. As children, our minds were stuffed with stories about gallant super heroes and cowboys who swoop in at the nick of time, dispose of the villains, and kiss the damsel in distress who has been saved from the villain's evil clutches. We were never taught to ask, "What about the villain? Don't they need to be saved too?"

We have been programmed, indoctrinated to believe that war and violence are a necessary part of life and society. Like Neo, the hero of the film *The Matrix*, we live in a world built of lies and falsehood. We cannot escape the lies of the world, because the world itself is a lie. When Adam, and subsequently the rest of creation, fell, we chose to follow the path of a liar, the Father of lies. Ever since then, humanity has been on a path of ever-increasing falsehood, giving demons and devils more control over our society, a society, they tell us, that needs to be built on a firm foundation of violence, fear, and power.

God's word rings clear: "See to it that no one takes you captive through philosophy and empty deceit, according to human tradition, according to the elemental spirits of the universe, and not according to Christ."[10] Christ needs to be our model. We must place Christ, the God-man, on his rightful throne as the Lord of our lives, spiritually, socially and politically. Every act, every belief, every ideology must be held up to the light of Christ and be judged against his ultimate model. He modeled for us the way of peace by first teaching us about non-violence in the Sermon on the Mount, then by physically acting out his own teachings by allowing himself to die an unwarranted death at the hands of evil men.

8. Eph 2:7, Col 3:24.
9. Phil 1:29.
10. Col 2:8.

"Religion that is pure and undefiled before God, the Father, is this.... to keep oneself unstained by the world."[11] But how do we do this? We have already been stained. Our minds have been warped. Our brains have been bleached of all truth! But luckily for us, Christ sent us the Advocate, the Holy Spirit, who dwells within us, purifying us of our depraved minds and giving us new minds, with new spiritual eyes, capable of exposing falsehood and recognizing God's Truth.

"Do not be conformed to this world, but be transformed by the renewing of your minds, so that you may discern what is the will of God—what is good and acceptable and perfect."[12] This transformation, this sanctification, does not come easily. When we become Christians, accepting God's free gift of grace and Spirit, we don't instantly become sanctified, aware of all the secret evil that lurks around us. No, we must work *with* the Spirit for our own sanctification. The Spirit itself was a free gift of Christ, but it isn't a task master, controlling our minds and bodies. It is a partner, an advocate, a helper for us as we attempt to walk in God's path.

The only way that we can have the spiritual and intellectual fortitude needed to begin questioning these "self-evident truths" of violence and warfare that our civilization is built upon is to live deeply spiritual lives. Only by maintaining constant contact with the Spirit that burns within us and other Christians can we fill ourselves with God's holy, sanctified truth and purge the ugly falsehoods that fill our minds.

The truth is that nonviolence makes no sense to our fallen and depraved minds. If we are to make any headway in understanding God's will for us, we must deny ourselves and confess that we have perverted our own minds by habitually following the lies that constantly assail us from the world. We must acknowledge that we are fallen, and that we need to be reborn.

Methodists, like the authors of this book, are famous for always talking about these things called spiritual disciplines. These are spiritual practices that draw us closer to the Spirit, that bring us into the presence of the Most High, where we can be remolded, recreated, and purified. Things like prayer, fasting, studying Scripture, discipleship and communal worship can maintain the relationship with the Spirit we need in order to keep our feet "shod with the preparation of the gospel of peace."[13] As normal humans, we are powerless to live lives free of violence. Nonviolence

11. Jas 1:27.

12. Rom 12:2.

13. This is by no means an exhaustive list of spiritual disciplines. This is only a common, easy starting list.

is utterly impossible for us to understand and perform. We must be born again, of the Spirit, transformed into a new creation. Our old self must be crucified in order for a new self with a new mind set on God's will to be resurrected in its place. It is here, in the quiet places, humble before our God, that the Spirit transforms us, sanctifies us, and molds us into the image of our Master, Jesus Christ.

Study of Scripture

The Bible is filled with many metaphors for God's interaction with His creation. A very humbling one is Jeremiah's metaphor of God as a potter. Jeremiah saw humanity as a clay pot in God's hands, marred to the point that our original shape was barely recognizable. He watched as the potter reshaped the clay into a new pot, ready to be filled and used.[14] When we place our marred clay selves, even our broken bits, into his hands, God gracefully forms each and every one of us into a beautiful, brand new pot.

There is a delightful modern song employing this metaphor that Jeremiah spoke about. In it, the musician sings of how he has strayed from God's presence and how he is now placing himself back into the hands of the potter. He prays for God to, "make me into something you can fill, something real."[15] The line calls upon the account of the creation, of God forming and filling the heavens, the earth, and the seas over chapters one and two of the book of Genesis. Chapter two's account of the creation of humanity records God forming us and breathing life into us, but the rest of the Bible records his progressive filling of humanity. It records how, as His chosen people, we let ourselves lose our shape, develop holes, and become ineffective for the purpose to which we were called.

There is perhaps no better tool for allowing oneself to be remade than through the study of Scripture. In the Scriptures, we find record of the many miracles that attest to God's glory. In the Scriptures, we learn of the goodness of God, how he has cared for and sought after humanity since we chose to elevate ourselves over him and force ourselves out of paradise. In the scriptures, we read of the faithfulness, humanness, obedience and disobedience of the people of God who have gone before us. In the Scriptures, we can see the holiness of God and we are confronted with our own sinfulness. As the writer of Hebrews put it, "the word of God

14. Jer 18:1–4.

15. Caedmon's Call "The Hands of the Potter."

is living and active, sharper than any two-edged sword, piercing until it divides soul from spirit . . ."[16]

As you read the Bible, allow yourself to be changed by the words of our spiritual predecessors. Listen for the still, small voice of God in your own life as you study the Scriptures. It will not be easy. You will inevitably disagree with God over what you have read. Study hardest at these times. Jesus told his disciples, "Whoever desires to come after me, let him deny himself, take up his cross, and follow me."[17] When Jesus says, "deny himself," it is often interpreted to mean ignoring one's physical needs. This is only a part of what the word means, though. This same Greek word, *aparneomai*, is the word used to describe Peter's denial of Christ, where he pretended that he did not know Jesus.[18] Perhaps when he said to deny ourselves, Jesus truly meant that he wanted us to disown our old ways of understanding, which our faithless surroundings have taught us. Perhaps he is saying that through learning about him and the freedom from sin and empty religion that he proclaims, our lives will be transformed in the hands of the potter.

Gandhi is quoted as saying, "You Christians have in your keeping a document with enough dynamite in it to blow the whole of civilization to bits, to turn society upside down, to bring peace to this war-torn world. But, you read it as if it were just good literature, and nothing else." Let's not only read it like good literature. Let's act as if we don't know our old selves and our old ways of understanding; let's get into the hands of the master potter; let's embark upon the journey of learning who we really are, in Christ, through the study of the Scriptures.

Prayer

Prayer is often overly simplified in common American church culture. Many Christians go about their business, praying when it seems necessary, only when *dire situations* call for communication with God. Lost car keys, sick relatives and Thanksgiving dinners are the few times in many lives when prayer seems necessary.

The truth is that *life itself is a dire situation*. If we have a proper understanding of the Christian life, we should recognize the need for constant prayer. As Christians, we've abandoned the easy life, and taken up the

16. Heb 4:12.

17. Mark 8:34.

18. Mark 14:30–1, 72.

cross.[19] We've committed ourselves to a life-long struggle against evil. Like Jesus, we need that constant connection with the Father in order to faithfully carry out the Christian lifestyle. Christ constantly found it necessary to excuse himself from his disciples and adjourn to a quiet seclusion to spend time with his Father, and we should, too.

The most poignant of these scenes occurs the night before Christ was taken captive to be crucified.[20] He told his disciples he was going off by himself to pray because he was "deeply grieved, even to death." Jesus, as he prepared to perform the ultimate act of nonviolence by allowing himself, an innocent man, to be killed for the salvation of those who didn't deserve salvation, found himself scared. He was about to suffer a terrible death, hanging by spikes driven into his limbs until he would finally suffocate. This deeply distressed our Lord, even making him sweat blood!

The truth is, Jesus didn't want to die: "Father, if it is possible, take this cup from me." But when fear came knocking, when living a faithful life became most difficult, Jesus knew right where to go to gain strength and the Divine perspective. It was in prayer that Christ found his faith. It was by conversing with God three times that Jesus was able to say, "Not my will, but thy will be done." Christ's body didn't want to be killed. But by speaking with his Father, Christ was able to overcome the will of his flesh, and perform the will of his Father. Not only did Jesus communicate to God his fears, but God, in return blessed Jesus with his eternal perspective. He showed him that the crucifixion *was* necessary, and that it was God the Father's will that needed to be done.

That is exactly what prayer does. First, it gives us an outlet to share our feelings with a Father who loves us. We can press ourselves into God like a nightmare-ridden child burying her head into her father's chest. Security can be found in confessing our fears and weaknesses. The Christian life is a scary thing, and we have a Father who knows and understands that fact, who wants to provide us with a warm embrace, a divine refuge from our anxiety.

Secondly, we receive something in prayer. Once we take the initial step of speaking to God, God meets us and gives us something in return. Just what and how much he gives to us is of much debate, and is probably dependent on the person and the situation, but the fact remains, he gives us something. You may hear a gentle whisper in your soul, or be led to a particular Bible passage, or guided toward a particular action. God may speak to you right there and then, or days and weeks later. In fact, you

19. Luke 14:27.
20. Matt 22:36–46.

may just wake up one morning sometime later and realize that there is something different about you; that you have found a faith you didn't have before and you now walk with an air of confidence that once seemed so far away.

How exactly God blesses us through prayer is irrelevant. What is relevant is *that* God blesses us. He equips us. Like a manager walking out to talk to his pitcher on the mound, he gives us what we need carry on and go forward. That's what he did for Christ in the Garden of Gethsemane, and that's what he'll do for us today.

The nonviolent Christian must "pray without ceasing" if he/she is going to be successful in living a life without violence.[21] Living the life of a victim for the Kingdom of God is too tough, too scary, and too difficult to be attempted without constant counsel from God. Just as Christ needed to pray on the night he gave himself for us, we need to pray every day to remind ourselves that we are giving our very lives for Christ.

Fasting

No spiritual discipline has been more neglected by American Christians than fasting. Somehow, none of us think to do it anymore, as if it's just some outdated practice for monks and priests that is in no way relevant to our own spiritual journeys. This is a lie of the devil. Fasting has *always* been a natural, accepted part of a godly lifestyle. From the times of the Judges, fasting has been an expected part of one's walk with God.

Christ himself fasted for forty days prior to his ministry.[22] It is interesting that Christ chose to fast in order to prepare himself for his long and difficult three year ministry on earth. He didn't choose to study the Torah. He didn't exercise. He didn't spend his last few moments relaxing with his family. No, he chose follow the Spirit's leading and wander a desert plain for forty days with no food.

It is also interesting that Christ seemed to assume that fasting would be a normal part of the lives of his disciples. "Whenever you fast, do not look dismal, like the hypocrites, for they disfigure their faces so as to show others that they are fasting." Notice that Jesus doesn't say, "*If* you fast," or "*Whenever the super-spiritual monks and nuns happen to fast.*" No . . . he says "whenever you."[23] He says this while preaching to a large crowd as he's giving his Sermon on the Mount. The "you" in this is plural. Jesus simply

21. 1 Thess 5:17.
22. Matt 4:1–11.
23. Matt 6:16.

takes it for granted that his hearers will fast in the future, and commands them accordingly.

But why fast? What does it do? How does it help us spiritually? Fasting, like all spiritual practices, is a bit of a mystery. There is something mystical that God imparts to us when we fast that cannot be explained. As two guys who constantly struggle to make fasting a normal spiritual practice, we acknowledge that God does meet us when we fast in a special way that unfortunately cannot be explained in simple language; it can only be felt.

But there are other things that happen to us when we fast that can be explained. Firstly, fasting creates free time. Much of our time can be taken up by eating, especially if we make it a habit to share meals with others. Fasting gives us extra time and space from others in order to pray, study Scripture and worship God individually. It sets us apart from worldly distractions and allows us to focus on the divine.

Secondly, fasting allows us to transcend the fallen world around us. Fasting is counter-cultural. It's stupid to the rest of the world. From television commercials, to bill-boards, to worried moms and grandmas, the message rings clear: "*Mange!* Eat something!"

The idea of not eating anything for an extended period of time (not necessarily as long as forty days, by the way), seems so odd and foreign to us Americans who constantly have food within arms reach. "We need to eat . . . right? If we don't eat every day . . . well . . . we'll die . . . right?" We who have fattened ourselves in this plentiful society need to be reminded that there are people in the world who must go hungry through no fault of their own. Fasting helps build compassion within us for the poor who have been victimized by those who refuse to share their plentiful resources. This kind of compassion is born through fasting.

Thirdly, fasting itself is an act of faith. It is unnatural for our bodies to go without food. Our fallen flesh doesn't understand why we would do such a thing to ourselves by our own free will. Our flesh, like the devil, needs to be reminded that, "One does not live by bread alone, but by every word that comes from the mouth of God."[24] We are forced to rely on God when we fast. We must have faith that God will see us through these times of trial. Skipping a few meals for a few days won't kill us, but it will make us seriously consider our own dependence on food for sustenance, which will then lead us to better depend on God.

24. Matt 4:4, Deut 8:3.

Fourthly, fasting punished the body, enslaving it to the righteous will.[25] Our fallen bodies can be the source of so much trouble in our lives. Like unruly children, our bodies are prone to desire unhealthy things, like fatty foods, illicit sexuality, and even violence. Like disciplining a tantrum-throwing child, fasting can help calm these desires.

If we are to live Christ-like lives, we must live as Christ did, which includes fasting. The cross-bearing, love-sharing, persecution-bearing life of a Messiah requires a faith that has been tried and purified by fire.[26] Fasting accomplishes this. Fasting strips away our pretense and our culture; it exposes our most animal instincts and appetites. Fasting shows us who we are on the inside, at the most base of levels, which is good information to know if we are to allow our inner selves to be changed by the Holy Spirit.

Nonviolence requires this kind of self-knowledge and faith. Without knowing what we're made of, without knowing what we can endure, we don't know how much faith we actually have. After forty days of fasting in the desert and overcoming three serious temptations, Jesus had the confidence in himself and in the God who sustained him through that trial that he needed in order to carry on with the rest of his ministry, which culminated in his selfless death on the cross. If we are to lead lives of radical ministry, where persecution awaits us, we need to know how tough we are. We need to know how tough God is. Fasting shows us just how much is possible if we live lives of faith.

Discipleship

The word "discipleship" has many different meanings in many different contexts. When we speak of it here, we refer to a kind of relationship between people. Christ chose twelve men, lived with them for three years, and poured all his knowledge into them. He gently shepherded them to greater faithfulness, keeping watch over their beliefs and behaviors, showing them the Way of life.

Such a relationship is absolutely necessary to build and maintain a strong Christian walk. We believe that everyone needs at least one person who they spend time with, grow with, and learn from. We need those people in our lives who are our spiritual fathers and mothers, who can rear us in the faith, teaching us everything they know about who God is and about how he wants us to live our lives. These people then need to help

25. 1 Cor 9:27.
26. 1John 3:3.

us through the struggles that are sure to come up when we break out and begin living by faith.

Christians need those people to know us, to know our strengths and our weaknesses, and to know our character and our faith. We all need someone who has already walked along the path we are taking, someone who can offer advice, correction, and encouragement. We need someone who knows the Scriptures better than we do, who can teach us how to read the Bible and apply it to our lives. We need someone to live out their faith in front of us, so that we, like a child watching a parent, might have a model, someone to imitate.

These things cannot be given by a preacher in a pulpit. These aren't things that can be gained by reading a book or listening to a self-help CD. This kind of teaching can only be passed on from one person to another. True Christian discipleship does not happen in a pew, it happens over coffee or dinner between two people who have chosen to open themselves up to one another out of a sincere desire to learn the way of Christ. True growth requires a seed and a gardener. Do you have someone tending you? Do you have any saplings of your own?

Communal Worship

For more than 3000 years, the people of God have gathered together to pay homage to their Creator. Communities of faith have always gathered together to sing praises to the Father, tell of his mighty acts for his people, and fellowship with one another, building each other up in love. Worship was at the center of Jewish life in Israel, and is likewise the center of Christian life in the Church.

We worship because our God deserves our thanks and praise. We worship because we need to be reminded of God's faithfulness to his people. We worship because we need to stand as one people, before our God, and pledge our loyalty to his Kingdom. In worship, we get to experience the love and beauty of God as a community, and in response, renew our commitment to God's service as a community.

At the heart of Christian worship is the Eucharist, the memorial and sacrament of Communion. There are many different beliefs about what Communion is and how it works for us spiritually. We believe that however it is stated, something special happens when the body of Christ comes together to share this meal. Christ meets us at his table in a special, mystical way that cannot always be explained. Somehow, Christ uses Communion to draw us closer to him and to one another, both of which are necessary if we are going to fight and win this battle which has been laid out before us.

There is a way that Communion benefits the believer in a much less obscure way, however. Communion is a kind of remembrance, where the crucifixion of our Lord is played out before our eyes and we get to physically partake of representations of his body and blood the same way we spiritually partake of the eternal life he bought for us with his body and blood. Through the Eucharist, we recall God's mighty acts of salvation, and Christ's ultimate act of self-sacrifice. As nonviolent Christians, we need to be reminded of Christ's self-sacrifice often, reminding ourselves that he calls us to that same sacrifice: "If any want to become my followers, let them deny themselves and take up their cross and follow me."[27] In Christ's sacrifice, we find our own sacrifice.

Celebrating Communion calls us to nonviolence. No eloquent preaching, no drama, no hymn or litany could ever express God's call to self-sacrifice and nonviolence better than the eating and drinking of Christ's body and blood. Everything that we need to know and learn about how to live lives that are faithful to God's commandments is right there, in the story of how his Son gave his life for the world. We need simply to imitate his model. Easy enough, right?

Imitating Christ is not even close to being easy. We are too fallen, too far away from where God intended us to be: living faithful lives of self-sacrifice. Much work is needed on our parts to prepare our hearts and our minds to be peacemakers in imitation of the Prince of Peace. Before we can fight God's war "out there," in the hearts and minds of those who are lost, we must first fight this war within ourselves, battling against our fallen, depraved desires for safety and security.

Fighting the "good fight of the faith" means pursuing love, endurance, and gentleness, and shunning all the darkness that dwells deep within us all.[28] This is the battle before the battle, the training before the big game. Before we can be sent out to war, we must first go through this spiritual boot camp, and toughen ourselves up for the dark days ahead, knowing that our training must continue even as the outward battle rages on. We must peer inside ourselves and confront the sin and faithlessness that resides in the shadows of our souls. We must root out our vices and hunt down our selfish desires. In short, we must crucify ourselves, believing that God will resurrect a new self, one that is capable of answering Christ's call to nonviolence. This is the Inner Struggle.

27. Matt 16:24.
28. 1 Tim 6:11.

6

The Outer Struggle

"We are therefore Christ's ambassadors, as though God were making his appeal through us. We implore you on Christ's behalf: Be reconciled to God." 2 Corinthians 5:20

ONE OF my (Jon) favorite movies as a child was "The Parent Trap." Basically, two twin girls, separated shortly after birth by their parents' divorce, are both at the same summer camp and realize that they are twins. They spend the rest of the movie trying to prevent their father's remarriage and get their parents back together. I thought the tricks and pranks that the girls played on each other and on their father's fiancée were hilarious! But I didn't understand the whole story until I got older. The maturity I gained through my parents' divorce helped me to understand the girls' urgency to get their parents back together. All their energy was spent on this goal. Nothing could stand in their way. Like the Gospel, it's a great story of determination and reconciliation.

In the same way, I didn't understand the real story underlying Christianity until I had matured in my faith. When I was a new believer, I thought that the gospel was simply Jesus-insurance against hell. I thought that a Christian's job was to try to get other people to see that they were so bad that they deserved to go to hell, so they would get their Jesus-insurance. I thought that good music and engaging sermons would motivate people to come to church and then see that they, too, needed Jesus-insurance. If only I could get them to believe and say a prayer of repentance to God and accept Jesus!

I shudder to think of the untold amount of damage I did to the Gospel in those early days of my faith. I did not yet realize how much more there was to the work that God has entrusted to us. One of the passages from the Bible that really helped me to grow in my understanding of this is from Paul's second letter to the Corinthians:

"Therefore if anyone is *in Christ*, he is a new creature; *the old things passed away*; behold, new things have come. Now all these things are *from God*, who reconciled us to Himself through Christ and *gave us the ministry of reconciliation*; namely, that God was in Christ reconciling the world to Himself, *not counting their trespasses against them*, and He has committed to us the word of reconciliation. Therefore, we are *ambassadors for Christ*, as though God were making an appeal through us; we beg you on behalf of Christ, be reconciled to God."[1]

As I began to understand more and more of what Jesus did by laying down his divinity and coming to earth, I realized how short-sighted I had been. When Jesus gave us the Great Commission, he told us to make disciples, not just converts. Conversion and belief in Jesus' sacrifice is only step one of this process. *Jesus came to reconcile the world to God.* A part of the process of reconciliation is the payment or forgiveness of debts. But it's *only* a part. According to the dictionary, reconciliation comes when a previously severed relationship has been re-established. Literally, when someone is reinstated to a body of people, like a city council, or when a broken marriage is healed and restored.

Like the girls in *The Parent Trap*, a Christian's job is to restore broken marriages. The marriage analogy is perhaps the most frequently used metaphor for humanity's relationship with God. Every one of us has at some point severed their ties with God and given him a writ of divorce. But God has said, "Where is the certificate of divorce? . . . Is My hand so short that it cannot ransom? Or have I no power to deliver?"[2] God has not left us, even though we have cheated on him.

Therein lays the Outer Struggle, the work of those who follow Christ: we are to help God recapture his runaway bride. Another Biblical perspective on this mission refers to the people of God as branches. Jesus said that the branches must be connected to the vine in order to receive life, which flows from the central vine.[3] Our mission is to make disciples, to help the peoples of the world, the various branches of humanity, re-connect to their Creator, the central, life-giving Source. To do this, we must become ambassadors, the representatives and the representation of God on Earth. We should live our lives so that those who meet us might mistake us for Christ himself.

1. 2 Cor 5:17-20—Emphasis added.
2. Isa 50:1–2—NASB.
3. John 15:3–5.

This is the point where things can get a little sticky. How can we look like Jesus when we have these awful, sinful bodies? It's true, the Inner Struggle can feel impossible. But, we've got a secret weapon. Jesus promised us that once he had ascended back to heaven after the resurrection, he would send a helper to us.[4] Through this helper, the Holy Spirit, God will help us change our outward selves to look like, Jesus, who is formed inside us.[5] Then, our lives will cause those we meet to be drawn closer to God. Then, God can use our actions and words to form Christ in them,[6] and they can start the process of working out their salvation from within.[7]

Most of the world knows that we Christians can run our mouths about sin and redemption and about how bad everyone else is, but seldom are these people the recipients of our love. What an awful state of affairs! Jesus said that his followers would be identified by their love.[8] How can it be that we are more often known for our judgmental attitudes than our encouraging words?

To correct this problem, we must all embrace John Wesley's challenge, "Do all the good you can, by all the means you can, in all the ways you can, in all the places you can, at all the times you can, to all the people you can, as long as ever you can." In the Outer Struggle, we must exhaust ourselves, giving each and every ounce of our lives to loving people the way that God loves them. Wesley's words echo Christ's instructions for how he wants his disciples to interact with the world:

> "Come, you that are blessed of My Father, inherit the kingdom prepared for you from the foundation of the world; for I was hungry, and you gave me food, I was thirsty and you gave me something to drink, I was a stranger, and you welcomed me, I was naked, and you gave me clothing, I was sick and you took care of me, I was in prison and you visited me . . . Truly I tell you, just as you did it to one of the least of these who are members of my family, you did it to me."[9]

This way of loving is completely different from the way the world around us loves. We've got to show non-Christians how much we, and God, love them . . . It's enough just to say it. When we let these ethics of

4. John 14:16, 26.

5. Rom 8:29.

6. Gal 4:19.

7. Phil 2:12.

8. John 13:34–35.

9. Matt 25: 34–36, 40.

love rule our lives, God's love will fill us and provide all the love we will need to give. It is Jesus himself who begins to work through us, reconciling the world to God.[10]

Dietrich Bonhoeffer described this concept in *The Cost of Discipleship* like this, "Jesus Christ, incarnate, crucified, and glorified, has entered my life and taken charge."[11] To allow him room to do this, though, we must be willing to sacrifice our selfish plans to advance our own lives and join Christ's selfless mission to re-connect the world to God.[12] When we fall and falter and don't feel like we can be like Christ, we need not be afraid. At those hardest times, we can ask God to take control and live his life through us. He will make us to be like Christ. He will use us as his peacemakers.

We believe that living our lives in imitation of Christ is an essential element of Christianity. The rest of this chapter will highlight and discuss some of the virtues that marked Jesus' life on Earth, and some ideas for how to apply them to our lives. This is by no means an exhaustive list, just a starting point for folks who want to be better peacemakers, to be more like Jesus.

Love

"The one who does not love does not know God, for God is love."
1 John 4:8

As I (Jon) was sitting in the synagogue, listening to passages from the Bible being sung in Hebrew, I slowly realized that I didn't know Hebrew as well as I thought I did. After two years of studying biblical Hebrew, I still couldn't keep up with it when it was spoken, and I was sort of frustrated. I attempted to follow along in my borrowed prayer-book and nervously adjusted my borrowed *kepatz*. Derek, my wife, and I were visiting the congregation of the Rabbi who taught my Hebrew classes. After a little while of being barely able to keep up, my mind wandered and I began taking in the room.

In what seemed to be the front of the room, I recognized the Ten Commandments on two gray tablets on the wall. I recognized them because so many of them begin with the Hebrew word, *Lo*. Basically, *Lo* means "not" in Hebrew. In most cases, it changes anything after it from

10. Gal 2:20.

11. Bonhoeffer, *The Cost of Discipleship*, 303.

12. 2 Cor 5:19.

a positive to a negative. For example, the sixth commandment reads, *Lo ratsach*, "You shalt not kill."[13] Eight of the ten start with *Lo*. Only commandments four and five are positive commands, "Remember the Sabbath day," and, "Honor your father and mother."[14]

As I attempted (with little success) to translate the tablets, I was reminded of how some of my non-Christian friends view Christianity: "All Christianity does for me is tell me what I *can't* do." In their eyes, Christianity is a drag, because it gives them a whole list of things *not* to do. To them, Christians are always either harping about how the Ten Commandments *must* be displayed in public or getting smacked on the forehead by a man with bad hair. Many folks have not been shown that Christianity is not defined by a list of "thou shalt nots." Love is what defines Christianity and love is a "thou shalt."[15] Love is something that we Christians *get* to do. In fact, it's the thing we have been made to do, our very reason for living.

Without love, everything else, even non-violence, is pointless.[16] "In Christ . . . the only thing that counts is faith working through love."[17] Jesus dared us to love selflessly and sacrificially; "No one has greater love than this, to lay down one's life for one's friends."[18] The book of Leviticus, the Apostle Paul, and Jesus tell us to, "Love your neighbor as yourself."[19] The Apostle John wrote, "God is love."[20] Perhaps the reason that God wants us to do the commandments is because when we do, then we're being good to one another and humble before him. Perhaps the best gift we can give the true God of love is to imitate his love for us, "Therefore be imitators of God, as beloved children."[21]

Since love is to define our very lives, let us not be confused about what Jesus meant by saying, "By this all men will know that you are my disciples, if you love one another."[22] Unfortunately, love is a very overused and worn-out word in English. Our obsession with romance has caused us to grossly over-apply the word. In America, we love our spouses, but ac-

13. Exod 20:13.
14. Exod 20:8, 12.
15. John 13:34–35.
16. 1 Cor 13:1–3.
17. Gal 5:6.
18. John 15:13.
19. Lev 19:18, Gal 5:14, Matt 22:39.
20. 1 John 4:8.
21. Eph 5:1.
22. John 13:35.

cording to a recent TV commercial I saw, Americans also love McDonalds. We love our children, but an NBA advertising blitz from the 90's also had the Muppets telling us that they love basketball. Tomorrow we'll love our cell phones and our collector cars. This is not the love that John and Jesus were talking about.

Even loving our enemies has become confused in America today. In an article suggesting that Christians should support a pre-emptive strike prior to the 2003 war in Iraq, Chuck Colson wrote "Out of love of neighbor, then, Christians can and should support a preemptive strike, if ordered by the appropriate magistrate to prevent an imminent attack."[23] In other words, Iraqi civilian casualties are okay, if the overall goal of preventing the aggression from Iraq against innocent American lives is accomplished. The thinking is that we're protecting innocent Americans and preventing Iraqi terrorists from making a move they would regret. It seems that to Mr. Colson, the defense of America is worth the loss of ten to twenty times as many innocent lives in Iraq as were lost in America on 9/11.

The first problem with this view of love is the implication that those people who *might* attack America and those people who live near the people who *might* attack America have somehow acted in a way that nullifies their right to live. Yet, haven't we all nullified our right to live by sinning and falling short of the glory of God?[24] With this way of thinking, we become forced to weigh the lives of innocent Iraqis against the lives of innocent Americans. As we go further down this line of thought we get stuck in a myriad of endless moral dilemmas: What if they are partially responsible for the terrorists' actions? And then if they are, what if they do some good things to make up for that small amount of support? And what if they *could* bomb us, etc . . . Whose life is more innocent, whose life is more expendable?

One simple answer to this dilemma is "neither, and both." Neither the life of an Iraqi civilian nor an American civilian is more important than the other in God's eyes, since he created them both. If our violence toward them doesn't separate us from God, why should their violence toward us separate them from God?[25] Moreover, the lives of both American and Iraqi

23. Colson, "Just War in Iraq," 72.

24. Rom 3:23, 6:23.

25. Rom 8:35.

civilians are more important than a Christian's life. As a Christian, you are to "love your neighbor as yourself"[26] and "be a slave of all."[27]

As a Christian, when we assume the goal of reconciling the world to God, we assume the role of the Suffering Servant.[28] In *The Cost of Discipleship*, Dietrich Bonhoeffer wrote, "If we are to share in (Christ's) glory and radiance, we must first be conformed to the image of the Suffering Servant who was obedient to the death of the cross. If we would bear the image of his glory, we must first bear the image of his shame."[29] Paul wrote, in three different letters to first century churches, that Christians should consider other people to be more important than themselves.[30] The innocent Iraqi, the innocent American, and the guilty terrorist must all be more important in our eyes, even if that means suffering because of their sins. We can't actively support the killing of any innocent people even if the killing masquerades as love of neighbor. We can get in the way to prevent atrocities, but we must not use violence.

The other problem is with the concept of "dilemma," itself. Bonhoeffer points out that Jesus had an unusual response when he was presented with humanity's very interesting, but very human moral dilemmas.[31] In Luke's record of Jesus' life, a lawyer asks Jesus which neighbor to love as he loves himself.[32] Jesus responds by telling a very famous story. The story is of a Jewish man who is set upon by thieves and left for dead. While lying on the road, he is ignored by two of his own countrymen and only finally helped by a foreigner, the Good Samaritan. Jesus tells the lawyer to go and do like the Good Samaritan, give of himself for anyone in need. "'You are the neighbor. Go along and try to be obedient by loving others.' Neighborliness is not a quality in other people, it is simply their claim on ourselves."[33] Like the Good Samaritan, we do not need to worry if the person in need is a saint or a drug addict, a pastor or a terrorist. We only need to help.

26. Luke 10:27.

27. Mark 10:44.

28. Isa 52:13—53:12.

29. Bonhoeffer, *The Cost of Discipleship*, 301.

30. Rom 12:10, Gal 5:13, Eph 4:2, 32.

31. Bonhoeffer, *The Cost of Discipleship*, 72.

32. Luke 10:29–37.

33. Bonhoeffer, *The Cost of Discipleship*, 78.

That is how God loves us. When we were his enemies, dead in sin, he sent his son to die for us.[34] We despised his care for us, did whatever we pleased, misused those around us, behaved selfishly, and ignored God. But his love for us is reckless and overwhelming. When trying to explain God's love to some thick-headed fellows, Jesus told a few parables, recorded in Luke 15. The first compares God's love for us to a shepherd's reckless search for one lost sheep. Our good shepherd is single-mindedly determined; he forgets the other ninety-nine sheep until his one lost lamb is safely home.[35]

To wrap up, Jesus tells the men perhaps the most famous parable, the parable of the Prodigal Son. When the prodigal returns after having squandered his entire inheritance, the father doesn't even wait to hear if his son is sorry. He runs to embrace him and kisses him before his son can get a word out.[36] He was too excited to have his son back to care what happened to the inheritance, or to make his son jump through any hoops to feel his father's acceptance. As Brennan Manning sees it, "The emphasis is not on the sinfulness of the son but on the generosity of the father,"[37] and, "God's love for us is outrageous . . . Not only does he require that we accept his inexplicable, embarrassing kind of love, but once we've accepted it, he expects us to behave the same way with others."[38]

This inexplicable love is exactly what is necessary for a peacemaking heart! Paul described it this way: "Love is patient, kind, not jealous, does not brag, is not arrogant, does not act unbecomingly, does not seek its own, is not provoked, does not take into account a wrong suffered, does not rejoice in unrighteousness, but rejoices with the truth; it bears all things, believes all things, hopes all things, and endures all things . . . it never fails."[39] The love of a peacemaker is a kind of love that drives one to sacrifice everything, even one's own life, for the object of the love.

This verse is often quoted at weddings and in marriage counseling sessions. Unfortunately, many of us don't even love our spouses self-sacrificially. Even if we do, most folks will still only extend this kind of vulnerable love to their spouse and, perhaps, their children or immediate family.

---

34. Rom 5:10.

35. Luke 15:1–10.

36. Luke 15:11–32.

37. Manning, *The Ragamuffin Gospel*, 166.

38. Ibid., 167.

39. 1 Cor 13:4–8.

To be a peacemaker, though, our love must go far beyond our immediate family.

How far beyond, you ask? Let's take God's example for a start, "For God so loved the world, that he gave his only begotten son, that whoever believes in Him shall not perish, but have eternal life."[40] God loves everyone in the whole world, not just churchgoers and their families . . . Can't we? Jesus gave up his life for all kinds of scoundrels, prostitutes, tax collectors, politicians, adult film stars, pastors, bullies, choir boys, pro-wrestlers, weaklings, saints, Arabs, Greeks, men, and women. He stooped all the way down from divinity to poverty to declare God's love, beyond a shadow of a doubt, to the world.[41] Mother Teresa, following in her Master's footsteps, humbly considered herself "a little pencil in the hand of a writing-God who is sending a love letter to the world." As Christians, we must also allow ourselves to be used to show all people the same self-sacrificial love and compassion that God has shown us.[42]

Generosity

> "Calling his disciples to him, he said to them, 'Truly I say to you, this poor widow put in more than all the contributors to the treasury; for they all put in out of their surplus, but she, out of her poverty, put in all she owned, all she had to live on.'" Mark 12:43–44

Our God is a giving God. From the very first words which he spoke to Adam we can see this. In that first dialogue between Adam and God, God said, "I have given," twice.[43] This might seem insignificant, but what if it isn't? What if God is so excited about the world that he has made and given to Adam that he repeats himself? In Genesis 15, when God makes his first covenant with Abraham, God states his intention to give to Abraham and his descendents three different times![44] God gave food to the Israelites during their wanderings in the desert. He gave them the land of Canaan to live in, protection, and the Torah to guide them. He gave and gave and gave throughout the years, until finally he gave part of himself to

40. John 3:16.
41. Phil 2:5–8.
42. John 15:12.
43. Gen 1:29.
44. Gen 15:1, 7, 18.

die to give us an eternal connection to God through the cross of Jesus and he poured out his Holy Spirit on all mankind.[45]

A story from Exodus illustrates this giving aspect of God's character very well. After the people of Israel slipped into idolatry through making the golden calf, Moses returned to the mountain to plead with God for them.[46] While they were speaking, Moses said to God, "Teach me your ways that I may know you."[47] Now, Moses had been serving God since he encountered the burning bush in Midian, but God had not yet fully revealed his character or glory to Moses. In this chance to reveal his most important elements, the critical parts of his character, God chooses to focus on two things: his presence and his generosity. "My presence shall go with you, and I will give you rest."[48] God doesn't choose to describe himself as holy, righteous, jealous, angry, a judge, or anything of this kind. No, these are the two most important things that God wants people to know about himself: "I will be with you and I will give you what you need."

God's character is defined by giving, but he also expects it to be a priority for his chosen people. When he selected Abraham to be the father of his chosen nation, God told him, "In you, all the families of the world will be blessed."[49] Paul references this promise in his letter to the Galatians, arguing that God had chosen to, through Christ, expand the family of faith to include the Gentiles.[50] We'd like to propose that God meant this to go one step further. Is it possible that God was telling Abraham that he wanted generosity? Had he wanted Abraham to share from the bounty God planned to give to him? Perhaps God has chosen to bless the world through his chosen people both spiritually *and physically*. We think that God is basically giving us an ancient kindergarten lesson, "If you have, share with those who do not have."

A brief passage in which God spoke to the prophet Ezekiel about the destruction of Sodom and Gomorrah tells just how important our sharing is to God. In Ezekiel 16, God is using Ezekiel to correct the sinful behavior of the Israelites. Toward the end of the rebuke, God reveals something important about why he took exception to the city of Sodom: "Behold, this was the guilt of your sister Sodom: she and her daughters had arro-

---

45. John 3:16, 17:1–3; Acts 2:1–21.

46. Exod 32:1–31.

47. Exod 33:13.

48. Exod 33:14.

49. Gen 12:3.

50. Gal 3:8.

gance, abundant food and careless ease, but she did not help the poor and needy."[51] We were shocked to read that God's major beef with the people of Sodom was not in fact their sexual perversion, as we had been taught as kids. God says that he actually destroyed the city because of their pride, gluttony, and selfishness! Their destruction at God's hands came because they were rich and would not help the poor.

When the band, Caedmon's Call, visited India, they encountered the Dalits, a people who are prevented by their neighbors from drinking water from the wells. Because they are *not* Muslim or Hindu, the Dalits' neighbors force them to drink from other wells or go without water. They have to walk miles just to get water for themselves and their children. The plight of the Dalits inspired an album dedicated to these people to raise support and awareness. We'd like to share some encouraging lyrics from one of the songs on the album.

> You know I've heard good people say, "There's nothing I can do,
> That's half a world away."
>
> Well maybe you've got money, maybe you've got time,
> Maybe you've got the Living Well, that ain't ever running dry!
>
> Share the well, share with your brother, share the well my friend
> It takes a deeper well to love one another, share the well my
> friend.[52]

Each and every one of us has been given gifts by God.[53] Some are great and some seem ordinary. It is from these great and ordinary gifts that he expects us to give to our neighbors in need. When we see past our own nose to the needs of those around us, we realize that we must do something. Everyone is not wealthy or rich to give large sums of money. But, we should still give, even when we have only a little. Let us not forget the widow who gave her last few cents to the treasury. Jesus calls her gift the greatest of all that had been given, even though it was likely the smallest amount.[54] Mother Teresa said, "Intense love does not measure, it just gives." If your neighbor has a need, meet it as best you can. Do not measure or hold anything back, just give.

51. Ezek 16:49.
52. Caedmon's Call, *Share the Well*.
53. Rom 12:6.
54. Mark 12:41–44.

Humility

"God is opposed to the proud, but gives grace to the humble . . ."
James 4:6

The single greatest enemy to both the Outer Struggle and to the Gospel itself is the pride of the human heart. C. S. Lewis called pride the "utmost evil," the, "great sin." In Mere Christianity, he wrote, "Unchastity, anger, greed, drunkenness, and all that, are mere fleabites in comparison: it was through Pride that the devil became the devil: Pride leads to every other vice: it is the complete anti-God state of mind."[55] As one pastor we know often says, "There are two kinds of people in the world: those who know they're jerks, and those who haven't realized it yet." Although some slip into it more often than others and some almost never, we are all jerks now and again.

Our pride and our swollen egos serve only to get in the way of the world's reconciliation with God. We act like we can spread the Gospel all on our own; by our own hard work in building missions, or our creative presentation of the Gospel, or by our inventive arguments against other worldviews. We measure success in our churches like it is measured in the unbelieving world. Our vanity causes the goals of Christian service to become improved morality in our country and increased attendance at our churches. The focus that Christ gave us, creating disciples, falls second to building bigger buildings and having more fun on Sunday mornings. Our pride gets us to believe other things, too. Like the idea that we're somehow spreading the good news by passing a bunch of laws so that everyone, whether Christian or not, has to act like they're following Jesus . . . even if they don't want to follow him. We act like the grace of God and the work of the Holy Spirit on our hearts play a supporting role in creating disciples. God is not up for the best supporting actor award; he's the lead, the star.

So what can we do about this "utmost evil?" First, let's take Christ's example. Jesus was equal with God from the dawn of creation.[56] Yet he chose to lay down his equality with God and empty himself for us.[57] He chose not to rule over us, but to serve us by giving up his earthly life at the cross.[58] Through Jesus' example we learn that it is in God's character

55. Lewis, *Mere Christianity*, 106.
56. John 1:1–2.
57. Phil 2:6–7.
58. Phil 2:8.

to serve, to let his own glory be put on hold to help those in need. As Christians, we must follow God's example and be willing to "lower" ourselves to serve others. No matter how "right" our beliefs may be, we should remember that we are still at the mercy of God, and therefore no better than a non-Christian.

Another good example of Christ's humility is from the Last Supper, when Jesus washed his disciples' feet. As their master, he got down on his knees and washed off the dirt and dung from the road. Notice that he washes everyone's feet, including Judas, even though he knew that Judas would betray him to the authorities.[59] Jesus set the example for us to serve all, even those who betray us and those who are our enemies. So, how can this example of a humble lord change the way we live?

First, we can get over our need to feel like we're right, especially when we're reaching out to non-believers. We are not on some heavenly debate team. This is one of my personal struggles; I just love to be right. There have been many times that my desire to out-argue someone has ruined any chance of the spread of the Gospel. My problem is that I forget that the life-changing love of Jesus, the very grace of God, is usually what changes lives, not my arguments. God's grace is best experienced through the eyes and hands of a follower of Christ. Is there a supporting role for apologetics and theology? Absolutely! But the lead part *must* be played by the meek, humble grace of God, springing forth from our inward parts like a river of living water.[60] If we must have an argument, we must do so without anger. If we must challenge a belief, we must do so with modesty. If we must correct an erring brother or sister in Christ, we do so with grace and a humble heart.

Also, we must stop making our own plans and then asking God to bless them. We can't live as though God is uninterested in the world, except to serve as a celestial vending machine when the times are tough and we need a little help. God is NOT uninterested in the world. He is a father to the fatherless[61] and a lover to the unloved and unlovable.[62] He hears the cries of the broken[63] and mourns the spilt blood of the innocent.[64] Through all these things he looks at us Christians and asks, "What are we

---

59. John 13:11.

60. John 7:38.

61. Ps 68:5, Jas 1:27.

62. Isa 62:5, Hos 2:14–15,19–20, Matt 9:15.

63. Ps 40:1; Jonah 2:2.

64. Gen 4:10.

going to do about this?!" He asks us to partner with him as he restores and redeems the world through Christ's sacrifice. We must be humble and lay down our plans for our lives, making the choice to become a part of what God is doing in the world. We must wrestle each day, being willing to give up our own agendas to be part of the greater story being written by the master author.

Nowhere is humility more difficult than in America, land of the proud. Think about the lyrics of our patriotic songs. "Land of the pilgrims' pride," "I'm proud to be an American," and "God Bless America." Why do we ask God to bless America? The next line tells us why, "land that *I* love." Americans are surrounded by pride at every turn. We'd like to suggest that perhaps we Christians shouldn't say "God bless America," seeking him to do things our way. Instead, we could follow Christ's example and pray, "God, bless the world through me in whatever way you see fit, I am your humble servant." This means that we will have to sometimes accept defeat and loss because they have their own places in God's will. Being a Christian does not mean that we will always win or things will always turn out perfectly.

Grace

> "For the grace of God has appeared, bringing salvation unto all men . . ." Titus 2:11

We both really like to quote funny movies. A favorite quote of ours is from *National Lampoon's Christmas Vacation*. In the scene where they eat the Christmas dinner, the family asks their Aunt Bethany to say grace. Her response is an oft-quoted classic, "Grace? She died twenty years ago." We've found that some Christians and many non-Christians have as confused an idea of what (and who) Grace is as Aunt Bethany did. So, we'd like to dispel some myths about what Grace is and what it is not.

To get started, a brief story:

In May 2004, a video was posted on an Islamic website showing Nicholas Berg, an American businessman working in Iraq, being beheaded by a hooded man. Terror experts widely believe that the hooded man was Abu Musab al-Zarqawi. leader of the terrorist group al-Qaeda in Iraq. Two years later, an American airstrike killed Zarqawi and some of his close associates. Shortly after the news broke, CNN anchor Soledad O'Brien interviewed Nicholas's father, Rabbi Michael Berg. When reading the interview transcript, I was startled by Rabbi Berg's forgiving reaction to the death of his son's killer's. He said, "Well, my reaction is I'm sorry whenever any human being dies. Zarqawi is a human being. He has a family who are reacting just as my family reacted when Nick was killed, and I feel bad for that." When Ms. O'Brien pressed further, asking, "Is there a moment when you say, 'I'm glad he's dead, the man who killed my son'?" Rabbi Berg replied, "How can a human being be glad that another human being is dead?"

Rabbi Berg initiated forgiveness. He chose to forgive Mr. Zarqawi before he even had a chance to show regret or ask for forgiveness. I am reminded again of the parable of the prodigal son, especially Luke 15:20: "And he (the prodigal son) arose and came to his father. But when he was still a great way off, his father saw him and had compassion, and ran and fell on his neck and kissed him." The father did not withhold his forgiveness until his son had repented, just as Rabbi Berg did not wait to hear if his son's killer was sorry for what he had done.

This is the way that God forgives us. The actions that secured the forgiveness of our sins occurred almost two thousand years before we were born. Our salvation rests firmly upon nothing but the two bloodstained wooden beams of Christ's cross. As we have discussed before, God chose to make peace with us while we were still his enemies. At the times in our lives when we were headed to hell, he already had the plans in place for how we would get to heaven. That is Grace.

Yet, this flies in the face of human nature. When we're wronged or hurt, our natural tendency is to hit back, either physically or with words. We have this innate desire for justice. Look at the many television shows that are or were related to justice. To name a few: Law and Order, Law and Order: SVU, Law and Order: Criminal Intent, CSI, CSI: Miami, CSI: New York, Missing, NYPD Blue, Dragnet, Miami Vice, Hawaii 5-0, Magnum PI, The Shield, Walker Texas Ranger, the Rockford Files, Starsky and Hutch, America's Most Wanted, Bones, Numb3rs, Cops, Judge Judy, Divorce Court, People's Court, Judge Alex, Matlock, Sue Thomas FBI, Columbo, Murder, She Wrote, In the Heat of the Night, Hill Street Blues, Perry Mason, and Kojack. Our culture is fascinated with the concept of justice, especially our own view of justice. This obsession with justice really messes with our view of Grace. We want so much to see the bad guy pay for what he did. But "making the bad guy pay" is not justice, it's revenge.

If Christians are to be models of God's forgiveness to the world, then we must be willing to forget what TV and human nature tell us about the need for revenge. God risked a big part of himself to make forgiveness readily available to those who ask. As Christians, we must also be willing to risk when we forgive. In his letters, Paul regularly urges Christians to respond with forgiveness when offended.[65] Jesus told the disciples that when someone offends us we should forgive them seventy times seven times.[66] Their messages are one and the same, we should be people who are known for our forgiveness and mercy. Christians should be the forgiveness people.

Courage

"Father, if you are willing, remove this cup from me; yet not my will, but yours be done." Luke 22:42

I don't mind being called a coward for my beliefs about nonviolence by non-Christians. What does bug me, though, is when my Christian brothers or sisters equate nonviolence with cowardice. It is true that the Bible, especially the Old Testament, is full of talk about courage. Armies and generals are exhorted to be bold and strong.[67] Indeed, courage is critical for the Christian. In the New Testament, Christians are urged to both "stand firm,"[68] and "be strong."[69] But, when Christians are encouraged to be strong, they are to stand firm in their faith and be strong against the attacks of the devil. Courage is an essential virtue for a peacemaker, but not just your garden variety of courage.

It takes a different kind of courage to stand up and *not* fight back. It takes trust that although things don't always look perfect, God is working through every circumstance for the good of those who love him. This is especially true when we are persecuted. Jesus said, "Blessed are those who have been persecuted for the sake of righteousness, for theirs is the kingdom of heaven."[70] To the world, our nonviolence in the face of danger can look like madness or cowardice. What they can't see is the guts that it takes to *not* use our own muscle or prowess to win, but to pray for those who persecute us. The unbelieving world doesn't know the calm confidence which allows us to lay down our weapons and trust that God alone will either save us or save those who persecute us through our nonviolence.

---

65. Eph 4:23, Col 3:13.
66. Matt 18:22.
67. Josh 1:9; Ps 31:23–24.
68. 1 Cor 16:13. 2 Cor 1:24, Gal 5:1, Eph 6:11, 13–14.
69. Eph 6:10, 2 Tim 2:1, 1 Cor 16:13.
70. Matt 5:10.

Jesus modeled this courage through the cross. When he prayed in the garden, he knew that he was to die and be separated from his Father. In human terms, his death would raise many questions and fears: Will the ministry I started with these twelve men continue on? Can I handle death? Who will look out for my mother and my family? Is there no other way to redeem humanity? Despite all these questions and fears, Jesus showed great courage. In the Garden of Gethsemane, he put his life, family, ministry, and fears into God's hands and humbled himself before God's will. He chose not to resist his persecutors, but to pray for them as they killed him. He was not a coward.

Being nonviolent doesn't mean standing by when we see injustice. Mary Anne Radmacher wrote, "Courage does not always roar. Sometimes courage is the quiet voice at the end of the day saying, 'I will try again tomorrow.'" Christians are called to lives of quiet determination, making a daily sacrifice of their lives for the advance of the gospel. This daily sacrifice can mean praying for the oppressed and downtrodden or raising a voice so that others will hear and come to see their plight. When all else fails, it could require getting in the way between the aggressor and the victim. Whatever the cost may be, making the daily sacrifice definitely means responding to injustice through the guidelines that Jesus and the Apostles gave us.

Missions-Mindedness

"Go therefore and make disciples of all the nations, baptizing them in the name of the Father, the Son, and the Holy Spirit." Matthew 28:19

Sometime after the founding of the church, we began to lose the purpose of missions and evangelism. When Jesus gave the Great Commission, he told his followers to make more disciples. A disciple willingly followed a teacher with the hopes of learning everything that the teacher knew and someday becoming like the master. A disciple was not forced to follow the teacher; he was called upon and chose to respond. The disciples were on a mission to collect up those folks whom God had called and who were ready to respond. Then, they had to train and learn to be like the Jesus.

Along the way of history, the focus has slipped off of *allowing* those who had been called *to respond*. Perhaps it started with the decree where Constantine made Christianity the official religion of the Roman Empire. At that point, the persecuted became the persecutors. Those who had clung to their faith in the face of terrible danger no longer had to fear for their lives every day. Now, the state could require conversion to Christianity. The spread of the Roman way of life through the spread of the Roman Empire was linked up to the spread of Christianity. Sadly, many governments since then (like the British Empire or some conservative American politicians) have supposed this link between the spread of the gospel and their own way of life and government . . .

But imperialism can never be the same as evangelism. The Gospel spreads when the Holy Spirit brings to life the hearts of the enemies of God; an empire or nation spreads its influence through the deaths of its enemies. Although both imperialism and evangelism require war, the wars are very different. Imperialism imprisons or kills the enemies of an idea or a monarch, while evangelism saves and frees the enemies of God from their own sin. Imperialism is spread by the select few in power, but the spread of the Gospel is the responsibility of every follower of Christ.

Consider God's example for how he deals with us. Despite the fact that God is above us, better than us, and all-powerful, he chooses to *come down* to Earth and relate with us. In Eden, God dwelt down here on Earth with Adam.[71] God *came down* to wrestle with Jacob.[72] Later, God *came down* to Moses in the burning bush and on Mt. Sinai.[73] When Solomon had finished with the construction of the Temple in Jerusalem, God's presence *came down* to fill the building. Throughout the Scriptures, God has repeatedly *come down* to us despite his lofty status.

Then, Jesus, "though he existed in the form of God, did not regard equality with God a thing to be exploited, but emptied himself, taking the form of a slave, being born in human likeness."[74] The King of the Universe chose to lay his divine nature down, take on human form, and suffer for us. He chose to serve us like a slave because it was the only way for the Gospel to advance on Earth. He is the prototype of what we all, as soldiers of Christ, should look like. Each Christian's body is the new temple that is inhabited by God's presence, which comes down through the Holy Spirit.[75] Like Christ, we are to give our lives, our gifts, and our status (whether we're noble or nobody) for the advance of the gospel. This is the Outer Struggle.

71. Gen 2:7, 3:8.
72. Gen 32:24–30.
73. Exod 3:4, 19:18.
74. Phil 2:6–7.
75. 1 Cor 3:16, 6:19.

7

God and Country

"But you are a chosen race, a royal priesthood, a holy nation, God's own people, in order that you may proclaim the mighty acts of him who called you of darkness into his marvelous light." 1 Peter 2:9

ONE OF our main tasks in writing this book is to communicate that Christianity is not easy. We want to show that to have faith in God demands a re-examination of every aspect of one's life in the light of Christ. Christ's life, death and resurrection were too significant to be resigned to the margins of our lives. If he is "the way, the truth and the life" then he must have something to say about every aspect of our lives, not just how we get into heaven.

For too long, we Christians have been "compartmentalizing" our faith. We have not been living a holistic Christian lifestyle. Some of us only think about our faith when we are at church or Bible study, or when there's a wedding or a death, or when we can't find our car keys. But God wants so much more of us than that. He wants our lives to be focused on and centered on him, his mighty acts, and his teachings for how we should live our lives. When we pay our bills, when we're considering which car to buy, when we're going out to eat, choosing a mate, watching television, or reading the newspaper . . . God wants to be there. He gave us the Holy Spirit so that we might be able to live every day with him right beside us . . . or rather, *inside* of us.

Particularly, our task in this book is to challenge Christians to think about war and violence through the eyes of Christ, with minds that have been transformed by the renewing of the Holy Spirit, not minds that were conformed to this world.[1] For too long, Christians have just accepted that war and violence are necessary in a fallen world. This, many believe, is only a matter of common sense. We hope that we have challenged this

1. Rom 12:2.

approach to thinking about violence and encouraged our readers to think about war and violence with a critical and discerning mind.

However, we also realize just how difficult this can be, because we ourselves have had much difficulty in coming to this conclusion. Nonviolence is not an easy belief to hold, especially since violence has been so accepted among Christians for so long. A change of perspective of this magnitude is very taxing on the mind and the spirit, but it is absolutely necessary for our minds to be transformed and sanctified. Truly, sanctification is a violent process, wrenching our fallen and depraved minds around truths that no longer come naturally to us. We are all old dogs trying to learn this new trick we call the Gospel.

But we must never shy away from the truth. Our quest for truth and purification from the lies of the devil will oftentimes be difficult, strange, or even dangerous . . . but we must relentlessly and even recklessly pursue God's wisdom, running the race set before us, fighting the good fight of the faith, no matter how foolish we may look or sound in the process. Consider again Paul's first letter to the Corinthians,

> "For the message about the cross is foolishness to those who are perishing, but to us who are being saved it is the power of God. For it is written, 'I will destroy the wisdom of the wise, and the discernment of the discerning I will thwart.' Where is the one who is wise? Where is the scribe? Where is the debater of this age? Has not God made foolish the wisdom of the world? For since, in the wisdom of God, the world did not know God through wisdom, God decided, through the foolishness of our proclamation, to save those who believe."[2]

With all this in mind, we wish to turn our attention to a very important topic: government. Any cursory reading of a high school textbook will surely show that it is almost impossible to talk about war without talking about governments. According to philosophers like John Locke, mutual defense, that is, the ability to band together to make war against those who threaten us, is one of the primary reasons for the creation of government in the first place. That being said, we as Christians need to take a critical look at our governments, for whom violence is the first line of defense and security. So, we humbly ask you to read on and consider what we have written with the understanding that what we say may seem odd, wrong, or even inflammatory.

---

2. 1 Cor 1:18–21.

The Question of Politics

Governments are built, protected, and sustained by violence and the threat of violence. Therefore, as Christians, we need to be very careful in our dealings with the government. Any entity that needs violence to survive should be naturally suspicious to the eyes of a Christian. Any organization that gains and protects its power through bloodshed should not be blindly trusted by those of us who have learned that violence is not an acceptable answer to solving the world's problems. As nonviolent Christians, and therefore as pacifists, we are called upon to stand against the violence of the State, and to call it to repentance by being a model of God's peace.

We here in America, where the lines between religion and politics have been blurred, have an especially peculiar situation. Even though the American Constitution endorses a strong separation between Church and State, politicians have long tried to establish a pseudo-Christian theocracy here. Both liberal and conservative candidates and those who vote for them think they have the God of Jesus on their side. Christians have entered the political forum and seated themselves on both sides of the aisle, taking up the political banners of their non-Christian political allies.

So where would Jesus come down on the great American political debate? Would he be a Republican because he's against abortion? Would he be a Democrat because he wants to look out for the poor? Would he be a Libertarian? A Socialist? Were the 1st century Christians communists because they "lived and shared all things in common?"[3] Is democracy God's only ordained and anointed form of government? Were the founding fathers inspired by God to write the Constitution? These are questions that Christians in America have been asking for more than two hundred years. They have these pre-packaged sets of political beliefs and ideologies, and many believe that Jesus would fit squarely into one of them, if they could only find the right one.

We're not so sure that this is the right way to answer the question of God's political beliefs. In fact, we believe that Christ would have a difficult time accepting any contemporary political position and that Jesus would not endorse any of America's political parties. This is not, however, because Jesus wasn't a political person or because faith and politics have nothing to do with one another. We believe that Jesus was an incredibly political person who died a political death. But we also believe that his political beliefs transcend the ideologies of our worldly governments. Christ represents

3. Acts 2:44–45.

a higher kind of politics, a higher social order that favors weakness over strength, poverty over wealth, and servitude over domination.

We believe that Christ would scoff at and probably cry over the way his name has been used to endorse worldly political entities in the past. Think about the United States. There is but one single concept that binds our government together: *rights*. The Declaration of Independence, the Constitution, and all the Amendments are based on this concept of "rights." Philosophers like John Locke first made this concept popular, making the case that all humans are born with certain "rights" to things like life, liberty, and property which may be defended by force, even to the point of death. The framers of the Constitution were well acquainted with Locke's work and drafted the Constitution based on his philosophy.

But is Christianity all about rights? Didn't Christ our Lord have the right to live a perfect (and probably eternal) life without having to die for those who would never be able to understand nor show proper gratitude for his sacrifice? Was John the Baptist thinking about rights when he said "Whoever has two coats must share with anyone who has none; and whoever has food must do likewise . . ."?[4] Or how about Christ, in his Sermon on the Mount, when he said, "Do not resist an evil doer. But if anyone strikes you on the right cheek, turn the other also; and if anyone wants to sue you and take your coat, give your cloak as well; and if anyone forces you to go one mile, go also the second mile. Give to everyone who begs from you, and do not refuse anyone who wants to borrow from you . . ."?[5] Paul echoes the same sentiment when he says, "In fact, to have lawsuits at all with one another is already a defeat for you. Why not rather be wronged? Why not rather be defrauded? But you yourselves wrong and defraud—and believers at that."[6]

If these verses had been written by Enlightenment era philosophers (like John Locke), or by the founding fathers, they would probably sound very different. According to most Western Law, Christ did not need to sacrifice himself, but instead he had every right to live out his perfect life without being bothered by us worthless sinners. According to Western Law, as long as we have worked hard for both of our coats, we have a right to both of our coats, and anyone who happens to be cold and wet should work hard so that they can buy a coat, too, and achieve what we have. And sure, we have every right to defend ourselves against evildoers here in

4. Luke 3:11.

5. Matt 5:39–42.

6. 1 Cor 6:7–8.

America! That's why we have servicemen and women; that's why we have police officers and personal handguns in our homes. Here you're allowed to kill anyone, as long as you can prove that it was in self-defense.

This gospel of Rights has been embraced by the Christian world. But what we have failed to see is that it stands in direct contradiction with the teachings of the New Testament. This false gospel teaches that if everyone looks to themselves and to defending what they have worked for, the world will become a better place. The gospel of Rights takes the selfish idolatry of the fallen world and attempts to use it to form well-working societies. To be perfectly honest, this gospel has succeeded in forming such societies, but it has done so at a terrible cost. We now have entire civilizations of people seeking their own good first, competing with others for monetary gain and material prosperity. It has created an entire race of selfish and defensive people who believe they are acting morally when they first love themselves as they should love their neighbors.

The Gospel of Jesus Christ, however, is not a gospel of Rights, but a Gospel of Sacrifice. It is about giving up what we have in order to bless those who have nothing at all. It is about turning the other cheek, when the law says we can strike back, and giving up our other coat when the world tells us we should be getting a lawyer. And yes, it is even about sacrificing our own lives in order to point the way to *the* life, the one who gave his perfect life for us. We must mimic our Master: "When he was abused, he did not return abuse; when he suffered, he did not threaten; but he entrusted himself to the one who judges justly."[7] As Christians living in a kingdom where personal rights are the one divinity everyone accepts without question, we must subvert this anti-gospel and expose it for what it is: selfishness.

This is not the first time that Christian leaders and politicians have embraced a heretical philosophy in order to gain and keep political power. For the last 1700 years, Christians have, in one form or another, dominated the political landscape of Western Civilization. These so-called "Christian politicians" have always been less than adequate for solving the problems of the world, if not downright evil:

1. In 313, Constantine saw a "vision" of a Christian symbol with the words "In this sign, you will conquer" written beside it. He took this as evidence that the God of the Christians would secure him a victory in battle. Constantine, and his successors, put an end to the persecution of the Christians and even made

---

7. 1 Pet 2:23.

Christianity the official religion of the Roman Empire. It was not long until pagans were persecuted and forced to convert to Christianity.

2. This favoritism of the Roman Empire eventually led to anti-Semitism which finally culminated in the Nazi holocaust.

3. In 1095, Pope Urban II ordered the first Crusade by exclaiming, "Deus Vult," that is, "God wills it." In this attempt to capture Palestine from the hands of Muslims, tens of thousands of Muslim were slaughtered, as well as some innocent Eastern Orthodox Christians and Jews who wanted nothing to do with the conflict at hand.

4. Even the Reformation did not lead to a peaceful Christian Church as German Protestants slaughtered Anabaptists (present-day Mennonites) who refused to support their campaign for a protestant German government.

The *god* of this World

In the Gospel of Luke, the devil tempts Christ with worldly power:

> "The devil led him up and showed him in an instant all the kingdoms of the world. And the devil said to him, 'To you I will give their glory and all this authority; for it has been given over to me, and I give it to anyone I please. If you, then, will worship me, it will all be yours."

Jesus responds:

> "It is written, 'Worship the Lord your God, and serve only him.'"[8]

What is so interesting about this response is that fact that Jesus never seems to disagree with the devil's statements concerning the authority he has been given over the governments of the world! Christ never says, "NO! You do not have this authority!" He simply responds by stating that he will not worship the devil because God's law demands that only Yahweh be worshiped.[9]

8. Luke 4:5–8.
9. Deut 6:13.

Paul, when speaking of unbelievers, says this, "In their case the god of this world has blinded the minds of the unbelievers."[10] You may have just asked yourself why the word "god" was not capitalized here. Check your Bible at home; we assure you that it isn't capitalized there either. Why? Because Paul is talking about a "god" other than Yahweh, a spiritual being that rules this world and who has the power to blind minds to the glory of Christ.

This same idea shows up in a passage from Ephesians, which mentioned in Chapter 1:

> "For our struggle is not against flesh and blood, but against the *rulers*, against the *authorities*, against the cosmic powers of this present darkness, against the spiritual forces of evil in the heavenly places."[11]

It is evident from the passage and its context that Paul is speaking of some sort of spiritual beings, demons even, that have won control of this world. But why does he use the terms "rulers" and "authorities" to describe these beings? Why not something worse sounding like "evil spirits" or "devils" or "trolls" or something? What is the point that Jesus and Paul are trying to make?

Their point is not an easy one for Christians to accept, especially in a nation where patriotism and religion are so closely tied to one another. (But as we have said throughout this whole book, the job of the Christian is to expand his or her mind to accept truths that go against our common sense: "Do not be conformed to this world but rather be transformed by the renewing of your minds."[12]) Their point is simply that *the world is ruled by the devil and his demons.* Sometime long ago, for some unknown reason, Satan, the great deceiver, came to power in the world and has been ruling secular and pagan governments ever since.

So all we have to do is get the "Satan-led" leaders out of office and install Godly ones, right? Unfortunately for all of us, it isn't that simple. Ever since Satan was expelled from Heaven, the earth has been ruled by a god who continually wages war against the true God. This is a truth that simply does not change. By becoming a worldly political leader, a Christian makes him/herself part of an already evil and irredeemable system. Many believe that if we only have enough Christian senators, enough Christian mayors, and a strongly evangelical President, we can redeem our nation

10. 2 Cor 4:4.

11. Eph 6:12—Emphasis added.

12. Rom 12:2.

and call it to repentance. This is the wrong approach. By allying ourselves with a worldly government, a secular government that is based on the selfish concept of "rights", a government that uses guns and clubs to enforce its laws, we become part of the problem. All of these Christian men and women will inevitably be corrupted by the evil around them. When we are part of a government we are forced to play by the government's rules, rules that are not based on Christ's death and resurrection, rules that do not understand grace and mercy, rules that ultimately favor the powerful and the wealthy.

So what is the answer to the political question? If the world is evil, how do we make it better? If we can't do it through power, then how do we do it?

The Kingdom of God

We would like to start answering that question by asking our readers a question of our own: What is the "Gospel" or "Good News?" When asked this question, most Americans would probably say something about Christ dying to pay the penalty for our sin in our place, thus securing for us a spot in Heaven for all eternity. They might even quote a Bible verse like John 3:16, "For God so loved the world that he gave his one and only Son so that whoever believed in him would not perish, but have eternal life." Others might quote Romans 10:9, "If you confess with your lips that Jesus is Lord and believe in your heart that God raised him from the dead, you will be saved."

We don't doubt that the atonement for sin is an important part of the Gospel of Jesus Christ. But it is much too shallow to think that this one concept contained in these two verses completely summarizes the "Gospel." In order to define gospel, we need to do a little concordance work, that is, we need to see where and how it is most often used in Scripture to help us better understand its meaning. So here is a short list of places where the word "gospel" or "good news" is used in the Gospels:

1. Matthew 4:23—Jesus went throughout Galilee, teaching in their synagogues and proclaiming the good news of the kingdom and curing every disease and every sickness among the people.

2. Matthew 10:7—"As you go proclaim the good news, 'The kingdom of heaven has come near.'"

3. Mark 1:15—"The time is fulfilled, and the kingdom of God has come near; repent and believe in the good news."

4. Luke 4:43—But he said to them, "I must proclaim the good
news of the kingdom of God to the other cities also, for I was
sent for this purpose."

Do you see anything peculiar about these verses? Notice that not
only do the words "good news" appear in every one of these passages, but
also the word "kingdom." In fact, there are nine instances of these words
finding themselves in the same verse in the synoptic Gospels and the book
of Acts. Look again at Jesus' command to his disciples in Matthew 10:7,
"As you go proclaim the good news, 'The kingdom of heaven has come
near.'" *The Gospel, the good news is that the Kingdom of Heaven has come!*
The Gospel for which Jesus and the martyrs gave their lives is about the
Kingdom of God. The Gospel which we are called to proclaim is about a
kingdom, a kingdom made possible by the sacrificial death and resurrec-
tion of Christ, a kingdom established at Pentecost by the coming of the
Holy Spirit, a kingdom ruled by God Almighty with his only begotten
Son seated at his right hand.

The whole story of the Bible is about the creation, fall, and redemption of this kingdom. The first 11 chapters of the book of Genesis document the beginnings of the sin that has spread like a disease across the face
of the earth, from Adam and Eve, to the violence of Cain and Lamech,
to the violence that led God to destroy the earth except for Noah and his
family, to the final sin, the ultimate showing of mankind's pride and arrogance before God, the tower of Babel. The story picks up in chapter 12
as God begins to solve the problem of violence and sin in the world. His
solution for this disease is going to come through a nation, a kingdom that
will act as his witness and ambassador to the earth.

First, we see God make his covenant with Abram, saying "I will make
of you a great nation, and I will bless you, and make your name great, so
that you will be a blessing." [13]It is the descendents of Abraham that will
grow into a great nation and be a beacon of God's love in the world. This
nation is named for Abraham's grandson, Israel.

But, before long, Israel becomes part of the very problem it was
supposed to fix. After God rescues the Israelites from their persecutors
in Exodus and gives them the Law to show them how to live, they immediately begin worshiping a false god. But they are redeemed, and God
eventually gives them the land of Canaan to dwell in. In order to govern
this nation, God sets up a system of judges who are called upon to settle
disputes and govern only when the need arises. This is obviously a rather
unordinary form of government, but it is built on faith, faith that God will

13. Gen 12:2.

be able to raise up judges when and where they are needed. But this faith is not easy for the Israelites, and they demand that God give them a king *just like the rest of the world* in 1 Samuel 8. Samuel, a judge and prophet of God, explains to them that having a king like other nations have is not so great. He tells them that this king will usher in an age of violence, that he will have many women in his harem, that he will demand lots of taxes from the harvest, and that ultimately everyone in Israel will be his slaves, which should have been incredibly offensive to the Israelites, who were once slaves of pharaoh.[14] Samuel ends his plea by saying, "And in that day you will cry out because of your king, whom you have chosen for yourselves; but the LORD will not answer you in that day."

But the Israelites remain firm, saying, "No! But we are determined to have a king over us, so that we also may be like other nations, and that our king may govern us and go out before us and fight our battles."[15] So God gives them Saul, David, Solomon, and rest of the kings over Israel, who all reign over a war-torn nation, a nation that is eventually split in two and that is taken into exile five times because of violence, faithlessness, idolatry, and failure to look out for the poor and oppressed in their midst.

But the good news is that God did not allow his holy nation to die in exile. Instead, he sent this nation his Son to complete the Law, to show them how best to live their lives, and ultimately to give his own life as part of that teaching, paying the price for sin and showing us how to love others self-sacrificially. In so doing, God redefined his kingdom so that it is no longer the physical descendents of Abraham, bound by ethnicity. The kingdom is now comprised of the spiritual descendents of Abraham, bound by their collective faith.

We read in Galatians, "Just as Abraham 'believed God and it was reckoned to him as righteousness,' so, you see, those who believe are the descendants of Abraham."[16] Peter tells us that the Church, the Holy Catholic (universal) Church, is the new nation, the kingdom of God here on earth! "But you are a chosen race, a royal priesthood, a holy nation, God's own people, in order that you may proclaim the mighty acts of him who called you out of darkness into his marvelous light."[17]

The Gospel, the Good News, is that we can be the Kingdom, God's solution to the problem of sin and violence in the world. Our participa-

14. 1 Sam 8:10–17.
15. 1 Sam 8:19–20.
16. Gal 3:6–7.
17. 1 Pet 2:9.

tion in the work of leading others to be part of that Kingdom was made possible by the death and resurrection of our Lord. He is our only political affiliation and we must pledge allegiance to his Cross, our standard, our only flag. We have but one ideology and it is neither conservative nor liberal; it is the radical, eternal, destiny-changing, life-altering, self-sacrificing Gospel of the Kingdom of God. The Sermon on the Mount is *our* Constitution, and the Beatitudes comprise *our* Bill of Rights.

Submission and Separation

To many of you, we suspect that this type of thinking is probably pretty foreign and perhaps even novel to your ears. However we also expect that you are pretty suspicious of what we are saying; how could we expect anything else? In fact, those of you who are familiar with the New Testament are probably asking this question to yourselves right now: What about Romans 13?

In Paul's letter to the Romans, he takes the first seven verses of the thirteenth chapter to encourage Christians living in Rome's capital city to submit to governing authorities:

> Let every person be subject to governing authorities; for there is no authority except from God, and those authorities that exist have been instituted by God. Therefore whoever resists authority resists what God has appointed, and those who resist will incur judgment. For rulers are not a terror to good conduct, but to bad. Do you wish to have no fear of the authority? Then do what is good, and you will receive its approval; for it is God's servant for your good. But if you do what is wrong, you should be afraid, for the authority does not bear the sword in vain! It is the servant of God to execute wrath on the wrongdoer. Therefore one must be subject, not only because of wrath but also because of conscience. For the same reason you also pay taxes, for the authorities are God's servants, busy with this very thing. Pay to all what is due them—taxes to whom taxes are due, revenue to whom revenue is due, respect to whom respect is due, honor to whom honor is due.

Yeah . . . you can see how this might throw a wrench into our belief system. "Why mistrust of the government if it is God's servant? The government is empowered by God to 'execute wrath on the wrongdoer,' and it 'does not bear the sword in vain!'" Why should we tell you to be pacifists in a nation of war and violence if Paul says that our government does not bear its sword in vain?

Well, the truth is that this has been a notoriously difficult passage for Christians over the centuries. It's difficult to make sense of the apparent patriotism Paul is showing here with the counter-imperial teaching he promotes elsewhere in his letters. But we see an interesting parallel between what Paul is saying here and an important event in Biblical history:

In the seventh century BC, a new darkness was brewing to the northeast of Israel and Judah, God's chosen, yet rebellious, nations. They had only just received a new sense of autonomy and freedom from their last imperial oppressors, the Neo-Assyrian Empire. The oppression they suffered at the hands of the Assyrians was not enough to call them to repentance, however, so God sent word to Jeremiah that he would raise up a new servant, King Nebuchadnezzar of Babylon, to conquer His chosen people.

So Yahweh sent Jeremiah and Ezekiel, his prophets, to call the descendents of Abraham to repentance, but they remained indignant and stiff-necked. They stubbornly held onto their idols and selfish ways, even in the face of persecution. But news of Nebuchadnezzar's swift rise to power came to Israel and Judah. The concerned citizens began planning defensive maneuvers to try to stave off this new attack from an even more powerful imperial threat.

However, Jeremiah, himself a Judean, explains that resisting God's punishment by fighting against the forces he sovereignly placed over them would mean that Israel and Judah would receive an even more devastating form of punishment:

> "But if any nation or kingdom will not serve this king, Nebuchadnezzar of Babylon, and put its neck under the yoke of the king of Babylon, then I will punish that nation with the sword, with famine, and with pestilence, says the LORD, until I have completed its destruction."[18]

He says elsewhere:

> "Bring your necks under the yoke of the king of Babylon, and serve him and his people, and live."[19]

And elsewhere:

> "I am going to send for all the tribes of the north, says the LORD, even for King Nebuchadnezzar of Babylon, my servant."[20]

18. Jer 27:8.
19. Jer 27:12.
20. Jer 25:9.

How offensive this must have been for the citizens of Israel and Judah. Not only were they being taken over by a disgusting gentile idol worshiper, but they had to submit to him! They were not permitted to fight back against their foreign attackers! They had to sit back and take it, and obey God's . . . gulp . . . "servant"!? This was unthinkable to the rough and tumble Jews. They were a battle tested and stubborn people, perhaps capable of staving off Nebuchadnezzar's attack . . . so why would God want them to rest under a foreign power?

Our guess is that God had two purposes in his call for Israel and Judah's nonviolence and submission under their pagan oppressors:

Firstly, he was teaching them to forsake their false gods by teaching them to have faith in the one true God for their safety and eventual return from exile. The Judeans and Israelites needed to learn to trust and have faith in the covenant made by their God. This is what prompted Jeremiah to write, "Blessed are those who trust in the LORD, whose trust is in the LORD. They shall be like a tree planted by water, sending out its roots by the stream. It shall not fear when heat comes, in the year of drought it is not anxious, and it does not cease to bear fruit."[21] God's chosen people needed to learn to have faith in their God even when things seem dark . . . darker than they had ever been.

Secondly, they were to become a light to the nations, demonstrating God's faithfulness before others by their own faithfulness in God.

Nebuchadnezzar was a brilliant general who employed a brilliant strategy for conquering foreign peoples: he would go to their capital city and take anyone of consequence, any leaders, teachers or important religious men and appoint them throughout his empire. This way, the conquered nation would be left without its leaders, cutting off the possibility of a popular uprising against Babylon. The Babylonian empire also enjoyed the benefits of a large influx of well-educated, charismatic leaders.

Knowing that his people would be dispersed throughout the empire in this way, God may have allowed them to be conquered so that they could fulfill their original purpose, being a light to the whole world! They would be able to speak of God's greatness and faithfulness to foreign people, teaching them God's Torah, his plan for how people should live their lives. It may very well be that God told them to submit to their pagan captors so that he could use them to minister to a lost, depraved people!

It is within this ancient Jewish tradition that we came to understand Paul's words in Romans 13. You see, by calling Christians in Rome to submission, God is actually calling his people to nonresistance and non-

21. Jer 17:7–8.

violence! The Jews of Jesus' time had a severe *hate* for the Romans. They saw the Romans much in the same way as Iraqi insurgents see America, as an unwanted, unholy occupying force. There was a very large faction of Jews called Zealots who felt it was their duty to free God's nation from this foreign invader.

Paul's words to the Jews-turned-Christians living in Rome would have sounded just as ridiculous as Jeremiah's words to the Israelites as they prepared for war with Babylon. In writing Romans 13:1–7, Paul was telling the Christians to avoid violence and revolution and not to strike out on their own. They were to be in the world, to live in the midst of their oppressors and to be a light to the dark and pagan Roman Empire.

Paul is *not* calling the Christian to patriotism; he is not calling Christians into military service to execute wrath on "wrongdoers"; he is not calling them to reform the empire by becoming part of it. No . . . he's calling for just the opposite! By telling Christians to submit to authorities, to refrain from armed rebellion and resistance, he calls them to be *separate from* the governing authorities. He is setting up a dichotomy between those in power and the Christians, whom God has chosen for weakness and submission.

The good news is that God's grace is for the humble and that his allegiance is to the weak, while his judgment is reserved for the mighty. God went on to free Israel once their lesson had been learned, and he went on to judge Babylon for raging against Israel, even though he used Babylon's disobedience to teach his people a lesson.

The book of Revelation carries a similar message. John was writing in a time when Christians were being killed for not paying homage to the Roman Emperor Domition, for not burning incense at his altar and not calling him "Lord God Domition."[22] In the midst of their pain, God gave John a message of hope to deliver to persecuted Christians. The message was that their oppressor, Rome, Babylon, the Great Whore, the Beast, by whatever name, will some day have to answer for its arrogance and its crimes against the people of God. By using so many names for Rome in the book of Revelation, including names that have been ascribed to other empires in the past, John seems to be saying that all empires will some day come under the judgment of God for their pride, and they shall be cast into the "lake of fire," just like in Revelation 19.

This is why it is so important for Christians to draw a line between themselves and the state they submit to. Empires will always become power

---

22. This is why Christ is typically referred to as "Lord God" in the book of Revelation. This is John's way of telling his readers who the real Lord and God is!.

hungry; they will always lust for domination and wealth. As Christians we can have no part of this, and we must minister to those involved with the Empire by being God's examples of how people ought to live their lives. We must show them true life, as it is practiced in the peaceful colonies of the Kingdom of Heaven. Even as we live under their yoke, we must invite them to take on the yoke (the cross) of Christ, and to become true citizens of God's holy nation.

You see, there are so many here in America who do not want to draw this line. There are many who feel that if Christians become part of the Empire, if they can take seats of authority, then they can help reform this depraved nation we call the United States. What conservative Christians and their liberal counterparts are doing is tantamount to the Zealots' calls for revolution! Winning congressional seats and presidential campaigns is *not* living in submission to the governing authorities; it is *not* having faith that God is looking out for the welfare of his people.

By rising to power, taking control, and becoming part of the Empire, political Christians are opening themselves up to all the temptations that power leads to, the most heinous of which is pride. This is not the place of the Church. The place of the Church is on the bottom, in the gutter, the floor-mat of the world, gently, humbly, and peacefully calling the world to repentance and reconciliation with God from the bottom up, never from the top down.

Political Christians fail to realize that the spread of the Gospel does not work like Reagan-omics. Many Christians currently in power in the United States earnestly believe that by passing laws that require Christian-esque behavior from Americans, the nation will gradually "turn back to God" and become, in essence, God's Kingdom here on earth. They think that morality will "trickle-down" from the elite to the rest of the nation. What these leaders fail to realize is that Christ came into the world to eat with sinners, to befriend prostitutes and tax collectors, to form relationships with those on the margins of society, the victims of the empire they found themselves within. By siding with the wealthy and the powerful, many Christians in today's world have forgotten that God humbles the proud yet gives grace to the humble, that Christ will someday cast Babylon and Rome into the fire, but will bless the poor in spirit, those who mourn, the meek, those who hunger and thirst for righteousness, the merciful, the pure in heart, the peacemakers and those who are persecuted for his sake.

8

Fighting the Good Fight

"Fight the good fight of the faith; take hold of the eternal life to which you were called when you made the good confession in the presence of many witnesses." 1 Timothy 6:12

ONE IMPORTANT question still remains to be answered . . . "How do we, Christians in 21st Century America, fight the *real war on terror?*" If we can't fight against evil with weapons, if we can't kill evil-doers, if we can't even take positions of authority and legislate against them, what can we do?

Should we stage protests like the nonviolent hippies of the sixties? Should we arrange sit-ins and marches like Gandhi and Martin Luther King, Jr.? Well . . . maybe. We would say that none of these are particularly bad options. But we must also realize that, as Christians, we will have very distinctive and odd solutions to the problems that the world so quickly answers with violence.

But before we can begin to answer the problem of how we should fight the terror in our land and in our world, we must first investigate and understand the source of that terror, the fear that drives us to violence, hatred, wagon-circling and gun drawing.

After winning World War II, it became clear that the United States was on the fast track to being the most powerful and prosperous nation on the planet. We believe that defense of this prosperity has been a chief cause of all our wars since. We're sure you've heard the phrases used to defend America's greedy foreign policy before, terms like "our national interest" and "the American way of life." Americans by and large think that the way we live is the greatest way anyone could possibly live. Many believe that America is the lone free nation in the world and that its capitalism and democracy make it a beacon for the nations. Most of all, many believe that our "God blessed" American culture must be defended at all costs.

But our question is this, why do Christians care so much about the American way of life? From a Christian perspective, why is it worth defending? Is it because America is prosperous? Didn't Christ say, "Blessed are the poor"? Didn't James say, "Come now, you rich people, weep and wail for the miseries that are coming to you"? Should Christians really be trying to build a wealthy and prosperous empire? Are there any places in the Bible where God's blessing is actually *with* an affluent, powerful empire?!

No? Well, then the American way of life must be worth defending because of freedom. I mean, we're all free here aren't we? Sure, I guess, but free to do what? Free to compete economically with our neighbors? Free to alienate our families by working late hours into the night, then trying to make up for it by taking the kids to Disney World once every couple of years? Free to build ridiculously large and expensive houses while we spend most of our time in our cramped cubicles and suffocating offices anyway? Free to buy four-wheel drive status symbols that guzzle gasoline and pour greenhouse gases into our atmosphere while we drive our children from one frivolous youth activity to another? Free to spend what precious spare time we *do* have in a catatonic state in front of our television sets, or playing mindless computer games, or trying to figure out new time-wasting, family-killing ways of making money?

Is our way of life really free? Are addictions to money, oil, sex and entertainment really freeing? Is worrying constantly about mortgages and credit card bills taking advantage of our freedom? Is being hypnotized by advertisements and political pundits characteristic of a liberated society? Are inner-city kids who can't get a decent education better off than kids in China, Haiti, or India?

No, we think American freedom is a lie. Freedom for uninhibited materialism and limitless selfishness is not freedom at all; it is bondage. Those who are poor are bound by the wealthy, those who are wealthy are bound by their money, and everyone is bound up by the discontent that is fed to us by People magazine and the Wall Street Journal. Voting does not equal free thought. Climbing the corporate ladder is not growing in righteousness. No, America's brand of freedom is a lie.

As Christians we have to look around us . . . at the ghettos of our inner-cities where the cycle of poverty promises to plunge generation after generation into destitution . . . at metropolitan areas where the shallowness of high school still reigns into adulthood, where the kind of clothes you wear and the kind of apartment you live in decide how cool and important you are. We need to look around at our suburbs . . . oh God have mercy on our suburbs . . . where mothers and fathers devote their entire lives to their meaningless careers all because they've been told that they need to provide a certain "standard of living" for their children in order to be good parents. Does it really matter if your kid has the newest $400 video game system or if he/she has the stylish $100 jeans? We need to look at our churches! I mean, we spend tens of thousands of dollars installing escalators in our mega-churches, only to spend $60 a month on a gym membership where we go and . . . you guessed it . . . hit the stair master!

It is these things, more than Democracy, that the "enemies of freedom" don't want invading their lives and poisoning their communities. Sure, we abhor all the terrorist attacks and totalitarianism, but we as Christians need rise above the hype, above the CNN and Fox News spinsters politicizing everything, and get to the bottom of what all these wars are about. We think that if Christians took a good hard look at Muslim beliefs and the problems they have with Western and primarily American culture, we would see that their problem with "our very way of life" is the same as the problem that the prophets and even Christ himself had with the empires of their own day, with Assyria, Babylon and Rome.

Again, we're not saying that Al-Qaeda or any other terrorist group is justified in killing anybody. Those are evil actions, and deserve to be condemned by all Christians everywhere. The Muslim-radicals who commit these evil acts are NOT, however, beyond redemption. They are fallen men and women, tainted by sin, just like you and I once were. Just as Paul the Apostle once was. He was guilty of the most heinous act of all, terrorizing the young, pure, loving Church, killing Christians and stirring up hate and resentment toward our little movement. But Christ was able to get through to Paul; he was able to break through the cloud of evil, to remove the hate-tinted scales from his eyes, and write the Gospel of Peace on his heart. Let's always remember Paul's words, "Christ came into the world to save sinners, of whom I am the foremost."

You see, when we kill others in defense of our "righteous" way of life, we forget this verse, we forget Paul's story, we forget the humanity of our enemies, we forget God's love for them, and we forget about their capacity for love. Of all the terrorists and civilians who have died at the hands of American Christians, how many future Paul's were there? How many could have been reached with the Gospel of Love and Grace and Peace? How many of these "little ones" did we rob of the chance of responding to Christ's open banquet invitation?

We're not saying that Christians shouldn't be concerned with terrorism or that the terrorists are somehow right to wage this war against

Americans. We have a responsibility as Christ's ambassadors here on earth to concern ourselves with the hate and pain that pervades our fallen world and to do something to try to alleviate it, without using violence. So if killing the terrorists isn't the answer for Christians, then what is? How do we wage the Real War on Terror?

Stop Caring So Much about Our Crap

Firstly, we need to realize that we *do not need* our nice houses, our cars, our clothes and our playthings. There have been billions of people all over the world and throughout history who have lived their entire lives with only a fraction of what we have, and have been quite happy and content doing it. It was Christ who said, "Do not worry about what you will eat, what you will drink, or what you will wear." Let's take him seriously.

If we stop caring about our economic standing, we'll stop caring about defending it. The truth is that the capitalistic system we are living in is based on fear and greed. Read the newspaper, a popular magazine, or watch a TV news show. Media companies are constantly touting American prosperity and whipping us up into a fury over perceived threats from overseas. If we stop listening to them about how great our way of life is here in America, if we transcend their BS, we cant stop being afraid. If fear is what drives us to war, then not listening to those who tell us to be afraid is a big step toward ending any conflict.

As part of this, we Christians need to be more vocal about our beliefs on wealth and prosperity . . . *especially to other Christians*! There is a very dangerous heresy floating around in the same Christian circles that have pushed for war with Iraq. It is primarily known as the Prosperity Gospel. In a word, those who purport this belief say that God wants Christians to be wealthy and powerful and rise to the top of the world in which we live. They typically refer to some Old Testament passages about the wealth of Israel and the prayer of Jabez to support this view. What they fail to realize is that this prosperity plunges most of the rest of the world into poverty. The rising in our bank accounts can only come from the draining of our neighbor's.

Let us be perfectly clear that we believe this to be a DANGEROUS HERESY! Paul even treats it as such in 1Timothy 6, when he calls out those who imagine "that godliness is a means of gain." He goes on to say, "But those who want to be rich fall into temptation and are trapped by many senseless and harmful desires that plunge people into ruin and destruction. For the love of money is a root of all kinds of evil, and in their eagerness to be rich some have wandered away from the faith and pierced themselves with many pains." You see, the more stuff we have, the more scared we are that someone will take it from us and the more we want to defend what we have. The more we want to defend it, the more we likely we are to fight or support war.

This whole diversion of our crap and using violence to defend it is more dangerous than just giving us an excuse to be violent. It causes us to become pre-occupied with the stuff instead of with people. Using violence only causes those around us to be afraid of taking our stuff, it doesn't take away their desire to take it. We need to remember that Jesus commanded us to make disciples of those we meet. However, with the threat of violence as a defense of our ownership rights on $500 iPods and $40,000 cars, a wall is built between Christians and those who we have been sent to teach.

Building Communities of Faith

Secondly, in order to accomplish this task, we believe the American Church needs to start growing close-knit communities of faith. You see, the early Church had a clever strategy for circumventing the fear and defensiveness that comes with owning their own property: they "were together and had all things in common." It seems like the first church community in Jerusalem shunned the idea of personal property and that they opted instead for a community-based economy, where everyone had rights on *each others* belongings so that no one went hungry.

What would happen if our churches today began to resemble the Jerusalem Church? What would happen if we started living in close knit communities where we shared our stuff and stopped competing with one another? What would that look like? Some sort of hippy farm from 1967? Communist Cuba? Pennsylvania Dutch country? Maybe, maybe not. However it looks though, I'm sure it would resemble the radical Christian communities of the first century, where Christians knew they were at war with the empires of the world and the fear they employed. It would look like the Christians in Revelation, who John and Jesus exhort to die for their faith rather than be tainted by the evil culture of the Roman Empire.

Building alternative communities is what God's people have always been about! From the time God created a new people through Abraham, Isaac and Jacob, God has been about the work of building a counterculture here on earth, which stands against the empires. Egypt, Assyria, Babylon, Persia, Greece, and Rome . . . all presented the danger of assimilation to

Israel, the danger that Israel might become like them. And most of the time, Israel did just that. So God went a different way and built a new Israel, the Church.

Peter called his Christian brothers and sisters "living stones," being built up together into a spiritual house, a new Kingdom of God. But alas, in the fourth century the Church fell under the magical spell of empire as well when it became friends with the Roman Empire under the Emperor Constantine.

We need to set right what has gone wrong. We need to build places where people can go and be different, where people can excuse themselves from the hustle and bustle of our greedy, sex-crazed society. We need churches where believers can find a comforting place of love and acceptance, of mutual care and trust, a place that has been sanctified and washed clean of the so-called American Dream.

But this isn't what we have in most of our churches. Instead of counter-cultural, fear-fighting bands of brave Christians, we have churches that support and purport the American Dream. Churches that should be beacons of love and mercy, instead export greed and fear and hate. There are Christian pastors who call for war, even as they lead congregations in worshiping the God of reconciliation.

So in fighting this war, we need some home-bases. We need some headquarters where we meet and eat together, where we keep tabs on one another and raise our children, where we worship God in spirit and in truth, not in hate and falsehood. We've got to build Bible studies and accountability groups where we can tend to the spiritually injured, and where we can draw up war plans to get back into the battle. These should be places where we can talk openly about the Enemy, and where his strongholds of fear and hate exist in our communities. Once this happens, we can draw up our "war plans," the ways in which we, acting as communities, can confront terror and hate in our own neighborhoods.

Being Christ

Thirdly, in fighting this war, the only real war, we need to change the way we think about what it means to be a Christian. For a long time we've thought about Christianity in a fairly legalistic sense; we all sin and are therefore separated from God and Christ's death saves us from that sin when we have faith in him, thus securing for us eternal life. Now there's nothing wrong with the above sentence; that's a very biblical way to think about our story as God's people, but there's also something missing from it.

There is a theme that appears throughout Scripture that doesn't get much airtime these days: the image of God. It starts in Genesis, where God creates man in his own image, only to see that image corrupted by sin. Throughout the rest of the Old Testament, God is trying to help the people regain this fallen divine image. This is why we get verses like, "I am the LORD your God; sanctify yourselves, and be holy for I am holy." And also, "For I am the Lord your God who brought you up out of the land of Egypt to be your God; therefore you shall be holy, for I am holy."

You see, God doesn't just want us to be good people who are nice and caring; *he wants us to be like him!* That's what the whole darn thing is about! It's about God trying to restore his image in humanity. Israel didn't quite get this, though. God gave them the Law and the Prophets to show them what he was like so they could imitate him, but somehow the message never got through. So he took a rather drastic step; he stepped out of heaven and became a man. The artist painted himself into his picture.

Billy Graham is famous for telling a story about an anthill at his Crusades. There is a boy who steps on an anthill. Saddened by the damage he caused, he tries in vain to put the hill back together. He finally asks his father what he can do to help, and his father tells him that the only way he could help them is to become an ant himself, and show them how to rebuild their hill.

This is a pretty accurate metaphor for what God did when he incarnated himself, and his love for us, in the person of Jesus Christ. We had gotten the image of God all screwed up, so he had to step out of heaven, empty himself of his power, and become one of us, redeeming our lost image. You see Christ wasn't only a sacrifice, but he was an example, a picture of how to live and love like God. He was a picture of both who God is and who we *should* be today.

By thinking this way, that is, by thinking *incarnationally* about who God is and who we are, we come to understand how God fights the war on terror and how he wishes for us to fight it alongside him:

> Let the same mind be in you that was in Christ Jesus, who, though he was in the form of God, did not regard equality with God as something to be exploited, but emptied himself, taking the form of a slave, being born in human likeness. And being found in human form, he humbled himself and became obedient to the point of death—even death on a cross.[1]

1. Philippians 2:5–8.

That's the key to fighting the real war on terror: thinking and being like Jesus, personifying God's love to a broken and empty world through our own self-sacrifice, emptying ourselves the same way he did, humbling ourselves, becoming obedient, and finally dying.

Empty
Humble
Obedient
Death

These are scary words that most people in our culture despise. These are dangerous words that call into question everything that most people work for in our world and everything that they think gives their lives purpose and meaning. But we know them to be the life-giving words of the Backwards Kingdom of God. These holy words are the story of God's salvation, the very essence of Love itself.

Bibliography

Ackerman, Peter and Jack Duvall. *A Force More Powerful: A Century of Non-Violent Conflict.* New York: Palgrave Macmillan, 2001.

Bonhoeffer, Dietrich. *The Cost of Discipleship.* New York: Simon and Schuster, 1995.

Cicero. "De Republica." In *War and Christian Ethics: Classic and Contemporary Readings on the Morality of War*, edited by Arthur F. Holmes, 24–25. Grand Rapids, MI: Baker Academic, 2005.

Colson, Charles. "Just war in Iraq." Christianity Today Magazine, Vol. 46, No. 13, 72.

Dumezil, Georges. *Archaic Roman Religion.* Chicago: University of Chicago Press, 1970.

Eusebius. *The History of the Church.* Translated by G. A. Williamson. New York: Penguin Putnam, Inc., 1990.

Gonzalez, Justo. *The Story of Christianity: Volume One, The Early Church to the Dawn of the Reformation.* New York: Harper Collins, 1984.

Hauerwas, Stanley. *Dispatches from the Front: Theological Engagements with the Secular.* Durham, NC: Duke University Press, 1994.

Hippolytus. *On the Apostolic Tradition.* Translated by Alistair Stewart-Sykes. Crestwood, New York: St. Vladimir's Seminary Press, 2001.

Hornblower, Simon and Antony Spawforth. *Oxford Classical Dictionary.* New York, Oxford University Press, 1996.

Josephus. *The Jewish War.* Translated by G. A. Williamson. New York: Penguin Putnam, Inc., 1970.

Lewis, C. S. *Mere Christianity.* Glasgow: William Collins Sons & Co., 1956.

Manning, Brennan. *The Ragamuffin Gospel.* Sisters, OR: Multnomah Publishers, 2000.

Milavec, Aaron. *The Didache: Text, Translation, Analysis, and Commentary.* Collegeville, MN: Liturgical Press, 2003.

Orend, Brian. *The Morality of War.* Ontario: Broadview Press, 2006.

Origen. "Against Celsus." In *War and Christian Ethics: Classic and Contemporary Readings on the Morality of War*, edited by Arthur F. Holmes, 48–50. Grand Rapids, MI: Baker Academic, 2005.

Pew Forum on Religion and Public Life, *Different Faiths, Different Messages.*

Tertullian. "Apology." In *War and Christian Ethics: Classic and Contemporary Readings on the Morality of War*, edited by Arthur F. Holmes, 39–43. Grand Rapids, MI: Baker Academic, 2005.